U.S. and U.S.S.R. Aid to Developing Countries

PRAEGER SPECIAL STUDIES IN
INTERNATIONAL ECONOMICS AND DEVELOPMENT

U.S. and U.S.S.R. Aid to Developing Countries

A COMPARATIVE STUDY OF INDIA, TURKEY, AND THE U.A.R.

Leo Tansky

FREDERICK A. PRAEGER, Publishers
New York · Washington · London

The purpose of the Praeger Special Studies is to make specialized research monographs in U.S. and international economics and politics available to the academic, business, and government communities. For further information, write to the Special Projects Division, Frederick A. Praeger, Publishers, 111 Fourth Avenue, New York, N.Y. 10003.

FREDERICK A. PRAEGER, PUBLISHERS
111 Fourth Avenue, New York, N.Y. 10003, U.S.A.
77-79 Charlotte Street, London W.1, England

Published in the United States of America in 1967
by Frederick A. Praeger, Inc., Publishers

Library of Congress Catalog Card Number: 66-26574

Printed in the United States of America

PREFACE

The emergence of a large number of new nations
in the postwar world brought with it a "revolution
of rising expectations," the ramifications of which
are playing an ever-increasing role in the East-West
struggle. While the key element in this "revolution" is economic, it also has a highly political
character. Real and imaginary grievances are vented
against former colonial powers and complete sever-
ance of all, especially economic, ties often is ad-
vocated by radical nationalist elements as the only
means for achieving true independence from "neo-
colonialism." The consequent political and economic
problems stemming from this environment are compounded by the pressures of the "population explo-
sion," archaic institutional structures, and demands
to achieve the fruits of economic development rapidly.

The aspirations of many of these countries for
rapid economic development have placed heavy emphasis on industrialization and infrastructural development. Such undertakings, however, require substantial amounts of capital and technical know-how, resources largely absent in these countries. Their
economies are primarily agricultural and often of
the subsistence type which yields little or no surplus. Industries are few and generally inefficient,
transportation facilities inadequate, standards of
health poor, the level of education low, and under-
employment widespread. Most of the people have
lived so long in self-contained village communities
and have such meager incomes that they constitute a
poor potential market. All in all, the physical,
financial, and human resources in most developing
countries are inadequate to undertake the type of
economic development desired. Consequently, these
countries have become heavily dependent upon economic aid from external sources to provide a large part
of the funds to import the desired capital equipment
and technical assistance.

For nearly two decades the United States has been providing an ever-increasing number of these countries with substantial amounts of economic assistance under various foreign aid programs. Generally, the long-run objective of such aid has been to assist in increasing the rate of domestic capital ✓ formation and absorption of technical knowledge up to a level which can then be maintained without further aid, i.e., when growth becomes self-sustaining. But, as yet, none of the countries receiving economic assistance has been able to attain an effective rate of growth to enable them to dispense with foreign aid. Nor does such an achievement appear on the horizon. Meanwhile, political instability, or at best only surface viability, has become a prevailing feature in almost every area in which these countries are to be found.

After years of denouncing Western foreign aid as an instrument of imperialism, the U.S.S.R., in the mid-1950's, injected itself into this milieu of political and economic instability with an aid program of its own. The emergence of the Soviet Union as a major economic power and an additional source of capital has enabled it to present itself to the developing countries as an alternate economic model: a former economically backward country which had attained an impressively rapid rate of economic growth in a relatively short period of time. In contrast to Western insistence that the growth of free enterprise provides the only basis for real growth under free and democratic institutions, the Soviet Union has pressed its claim that only a centrally planned and controlled economy void of private enterprise can provide the desired social and economic development.

In this competition for adherents, the U.S. and the U.S.S.R. have employed economic aid as a major foreign policy instrument. But this interplay of economic and political objectives has tended to prevent an adequate understanding of the nature of the two programs (particularly the Soviet program) and the results which can be achieved with economic

assistance. The primary objective of this study is
to compare the contents, purposes, and economic im-
pacts of these programs in an effort to better under-
stand them and to assess the extent to which the
programs have served the professed objectives of the
U.S. and the U.S.S.R. and the contribution such aid
has made to the economic development of the recipient countries.

An assessment of this kind encounters a variety
of obvious difficulties. Perhaps the most important
obstacle is the lack of adequate statistical information in the developing countries. Data concerning
aggregate output, savings, investment, and consumption is limited. In industry, information generally
is available only for those activities in which
large factory units are important. Even more disconcerting is the absence of reasonable statistical
information concerning investment and consumption in
the agricultural sector.

Another important problem concerns the measurement of economic growth. Studies of this kind generally view economic growth in terms of Gross National Product and national income. But for the developing countries the use of such criteria leaves much
to be desired. A considerable portion of the output
of most of these countries either is consumed directly by the producers or bartered for other goods and
services and, consequently, does not enter the domestic markets or the country's national accounts.
This is particularly true in rural areas. In view
of these difficulties, any measurement technique employed can be no more than a usable order of magnitude.

As for economic aid, no precise definition is
possible. For the purposes of this study, economic
assistance consists of those resources which enable
an aid-receiving country to increase its imports of
goods and services without immediately increasing
the burden on its current account or foreign-exchange
reserves. Such assistance includes all grants of
foreign exchange, goods, and services; "soft loans"

provided in foreign exchange but in which repayments
of principal and interest are accepted in the debt-
or's currency; all sales of commodities for which
payment is made in blocked local currency; loans repayable in hard currency but allowing payments to be
deferred long enough and kept low enough to enable
the borrower to increase its capacity to produce and
to generate export earnings to service these debts;
and receipt of goods and services in exchange for
the borrower's exports, an exchange confined largely
to aid received from the U.S.S.R.

The developing areas included in this study are:

1. Africa, not including the Republic of South
Africa and the United Arab Republic;

2. Far East, which includes all non-Communist
countries from Burma to South Korea, except Japan;

3. Latin America;

4. Middle East, which includes Greece, Turkey,
Iran, Israel, the Arab countries of Western Asia,
and the United Arab Republic; and

5. South Asia, which includes Afghanistan,
Ceylon, India, Nepal, and Pakistan.

CONTENTS

Chapter   Page

LIST OF TABLES

ABBREVIATIONS

AID	Agency for International Development
DLF	Development Loan Fund
EARIS	Egyptian American Rural Improvement Service
ECA	Economic Cooperation Administration
EDO	Economic Development Organization (U.A.R.)
GPA	General Petroleum Authority (U.A.R.)
IATCP	Indo-American Technical Cooperation Program
ICA	International Cooperation Administration
IDB	Industrial Development Bank (Turkey)
IPC	Indian Planning Commission
MSP	Mutual Security Program
NPC	National Production Council (U.A.R.)
OECD	Organization for Economic Cooperation and Development
OEEC	Organization for European Economic Cooperation
USOM	United States Operations Mission

U.S. and U.S.S.R. Aid to Developing Countries

CHAPTER **1** OBJECTIVES OF
THE ECONOMIC
AID PROGRAMS

OBJECTIVES OF THE U.S. ECONOMIC AID PROGRAM

Our aid programs are designed to pro-
mote world conditions which will permit this nation to survive, to progress,
and to prosper, in a setting of peace
and its fundamental human values safely
secured.[1]

This statement by a staff member of the President's Committee to Study the U.S. Military Assistance Program (The Draper Committee) indicates suc-
cinctly the general objectives of the U.S. economic
aid programs. It also indicates why these objectives
have varied, often in response to international conditions which prevailed at a particular time. In
pursuit of the goals stated above, our aid program
has become a major instrument of our foreign policy
directed toward furthering our national interests.
As one study points out:

Since the end of World War II, U.S. aid
programs have included rehabilitation,
restoration of economic stability in
key countries, the supplying of arms
and economic aid to halt Communist en-
croachment, the rebuilding of the armed
forces of allied countries threatened
by Communist aggression, the encouragement of technical cooperation, the pro-
motion of economic development and the
expression of humanitarianism.[2]

1

Postwar Policies

The U.S. program grew out of a desire to assist our wartime allies to rebuild their war-ravaged economies. Assistance extended through the United Nations Relief and Rehabilitation Administration (UNRRA) was designed to cope with the immediate problem of caring for the people liberated from Axis-held territories. American military forces conducted similar programs in ex-enemy areas. In 1945-46, about $8 billion in credits and grants were made available to former allies to help them reconstruct their economies.[3] A concomitant objective was to rebuild an international economy in which economic growth, free trade, and convertibility prevailed. The pursuit of this objective previously had led to the Bretton Woods Agreements and the creation of the International Bank for Reconstruction and Development (IBRD) and the International Monetary Fund (IMF) in 1944.

By 1947, however, it had become apparent that the assumptions of Bretton Woods were unrealistic and the reconstruction of Europe's economy required a longer-term program. Moreover, international Communism was engaged in a program designed to expand its influence in Europe by exploiting the Continent's economic instability. These events led first to an emergency program of U.S. economic and military assistance for Greece and Turkey and, subsequently, to the Marshall Plan for Europe. The North Atlantic Treaty Organization (NATO) was created to counter the possibility of Soviet military actions against Western Europe.

The first postwar legislation for the specific purpose of assisting in the economic development of the developing countries was the Act for International Development, enacted in May, 1950. This legislation was a direct outgrowth of President Truman's inaugural address in January, 1949, in which he called for a "bold, new program" for all the developing countries; the famous Point Four declaration which launched the Technical Assistance Program.[4]

Actually, President Truman had outlined a much
broader program of international economic development, of which technical assistance was only one of
two principal elements. The other important component was capital for investment which would be provided by the Export-Import Bank, the IBRD, and private sources. There was no suggestion that the
United States was prepared to provide grants of
capital.

Response to Communist Aggression

But economic assistance solely for development
purposes was short-lived. International Communism's
political, military, and subversive activities in
the non-Communist world necessitated broader measures
to counter these pressures. The concept of mutual
security was developed, and its first manifestation
was the Defense Assistance Act of October, 1949.
The primary purpose of this legislation was to provide military assistance to those European countries
which joined the NATO alliance. Under this legislation, grant aid also was made available to other
nations threatened by Communism, e.g., to Greece,
Turkey, and Korea.[5]

Following the invasion of South Korea in June,
1950, the emphasis on economic cooperation (characterized by the Marshall Plan and the Technical Assistance Program) shifted to considerations of security. Resistance to Communist military aggression
became the principal criteria for determining the
recipients of U.S. economic assistance. The Mutual
Security Act of 1951 put military, economic, and
technical aid under one legislative authorization.
The attitude toward foreign aid which prevailed at
that time was summed up in the report of the Randall
Commission, which recommended:

> Economic aid on a grant basis should
> be terminated as soon as possible. No
> further aid is justified unless it con-
> tributes to the security of the United
> States. . . . In cases where our se-
> curity is importantly involved, the

Commission believes that moderate
grants-in-aid may serve the national
interests of the United States.[6]

The passage of the Mutual Security Act of 1954
set the pattern for U.S. aid for the new few years.
To enable allied countries to maintain large military establishments without substantial drains on
their economies, sizable amounts of economic aid accompanied military assistance. Section 131 (a) of
the Act authorized the President to provide countries
receiving military assistance from the U.S. or joined
with the U.S. in a regional collective defense ar-
rangement, with commodities, services, financial, and
other assistance necessary to sustain an increased
military effort.[7] This form of economic aid, termed
defense support, originally was conceived in 1953
and became available in principle to all countries
receiving military aid from the U.S. In fact, defense support became the primary form of U.S. aid.
The legislation did, however, provide for the first
time a separate status to assistance for economic
development. Such aid was made available to countries that were not participating in the defense
program, provided security considerations dictated
such dispensations.

Response to the Soviet Aid Program

By the mid-1950's, the U.S. economic aid program began to enter a new phase. Geographic emphasis shifted from Europe to the developing countries
and by 1957 it had become obvious that military al-
liances alone could not forestall Communist advances
in these countries. What was required was a more
positive and comprehensive policy, with economic development the primary objective. A particularly
significant aspect of this reassessment was the re-
moval of the odium with which the foreign policies
of the major neutrals was viewed. As the key countries of the areas in which they were located, their
development was viewed as essential for stability in
those areas. The subsequent massive aid program for
India, for example, reflected this basic change in
attitude.

This new emphasis on meeting the economic development requirements of the developing countries
was, in part, a response to the success the U.S.S.R.
was experiencing in expanding political and economic
relations with these countries. Alluding to this
consideration in testimony before the House Committee
on Foreign Affairs, James H. Smith, Jr., Director of
the International Cooperation Administration stated:

> The Soviet economic program is an im-
> portant fact and it must be given due
> weight in the formulation of our pol-
> icies. The Soviets have revealed a
> large and apparently highly effective
> apparatus. The administration of So-
> viet aid is of particular significance
> to the operations of ICA.[8]

Soviet Premier Khrushchev echoed this sentiment
when he claimed:

> This aid which the capitalist countries
> are planning to extend to the states
> which have recently won their indepen-
> dence should also be viewed as a par-
> ticular kind of Soviet aid to these
> states. If the Soviet Union did not
> exist is it likely that the monopolies
> of the imperialist powers would aid
> the underdeveloped countries? Of
> course not.[9]

Another important factor recognized was that
long-term financial aid to supplement technical assistance programs was necessary. It was the first
step toward increasing administration requests for
expanding the volume of long-term assistance. Moreover, inasmuch as such assistance would have to be
loaned for investment in projects of a social overhead type, partial repayment in local currency was
favored. The Development Loan Fund (DLF) was created for this purpose and a large share of subsequent loans during the next few years consisted of
such "soft" loans.

In 1961, the character of the U.S. aid program
went through another significant transformation.
Greater emphasis was placed on long-range economic
development plans, self-help, and mobilization of
domestic resources in recipient countries. For the
first time there were demands that the rehabilitated
countries of Western Europe begin to bear a part of
the aid burden. The Foreign Assistance Act of 1961,
recognizing the disadvantages stemming from the ever
increasing holdings of foreign currencies, called
for AID loans to be repaid in dollars, but with extremely lenient payment terms. Perhaps the most
significant change was the increased emphasis on
non-Export-Import Bank aid to Latin American countries to finance social development programs; a response to the threat of Castroism among the unstable
governments of many Latin American countries.

An important underlying theme of the U.S. aid
program (and one of the major contrasts with the
Soviet program) has been that the only effective way
of promoting long-run economic growth with U.S.
economic aid is to encourage the growth of the private sectors in recipient countries. One report
suggests:

> Development achieved under State di-
> rection absorbs more scarce resources
> per unit of achievement and cements
> fewer strong ties with the United
> States than development achieved
> largely by way of the activation of
> latent private resources in the less
> developed countries.[10]

In 1963, the Clay Report, commenting on the relation of our aid to our objectives, indicated that
too much U.S. aid had been provided to public undertakings and not enough consideration had been given
to the "interests of our economic system." The report called for expanding our aid to the private
sector, which "alone could make the greatest contribution to rapid economic growth and overall
development."[11]

OBJECTIVES OF THE SOVIET
ECONOMIC AID PROGRAM

Soviet economic relations with the developing countries form an integral part of over-all Soviet policy toward these countries. The rapid growth of these relations with developing countries has been synchronized with Soviet political, cultural, and propaganda activities. Soviet economic relations with these countries are, in the words of one au-thor, "as much a political as it is an economic phenomenon . . . a curious amalgam of politico-economic considerations which makes impossible any meaningful distinction between the two."[12]

But unless such observations are placed in proper perspective, they tend to obscure the content of Soviet activity and imply that political consider-ations must dictate every economic act. For Soviet policy toward the developing countries has its im-mediate and long-run goals, and the ultimate political objective may, in the Soviet view, require a consid-erable period of time to accomplish. The economic element in this connection is an important one and its employment in the Soviet pursuit of that objec-tive requires economic tools. To be an effective instrument, the U.S.S.R. cannot permit political considerations to continually submerge economic rationale.

Post-Stalin Change in Soviet Policy

After Stalin's death in 1953, Soviet policy to-ward the developing countries changed dramatically. The new Soviet regime saw in these countries weak economic and political structures as well as nation-alist and anticolonial sentiments susceptible to the expansion of Soviet influence. This assessment was particularly important to them in view of the rapid rate at which Europe's economy was being rebuilt. In contrast to Salin's militant policy which pre-vailed between 1945 and 1952, the new Soviet leaders launched a program designed to cultivate the Afro-Asian countries. Tactical priority was given to gaining entry to these countries, to establishing

a position which could be used to influence their
policies, and to reduce or eliminate Western influence. In the years since 1953, the nationalist governments have been accepted and acknowledged and
diplomatic and economic relations established with
most of them. Simultaneously, local Communist parties subservient to Moscow's directives have been
restrained from overt revolutionary activity that
would offend nationalist governments.

One cannot be certain that Stalin would not
have pursued a similar course, or at least assisted
those countries where anti-Western sentiment was
strongest. The "national liberation" of colonial
peoples and their absorption into the Communist
world have always held a high priority in Communist
strategic thinking. Stalin extended economic assistance to Turkey in 1934 when that country was developing its system of state enterprises. In 1951, the
U.S.S.R. offered assistance to the Economic Commission for Asia and the Far East and again at the
World Economic Conference in Moscow in 1952.[13] But
the large demands of the Communist regimes in Eastern Europe and Communist China for assistance in
consolidating their positions were probably an important factor which prevented the U.S.S.R. from
initiating a program earlier.

The U.S.S.R. provided some indication in 1954
that the expansion of economic relations with the
developing countries was to receive a high priority.
The number of Soviet trade and payments agreements
concluded with many of these countries increased
substantially. Participation in international trade
fairs increased and a number of small credits was
extended to Afghanistan. The Soviet aid program,
however, did not blossom forth until 1955, when major aid agreements were concluded with Afghanistan,
Burma, India, and Indonesia. The initial willingness of the U.S.S.R. to dispense economic aid to the
developing countries was motivated by a desire to
gain recognition as a world power and to foster neutralism by the developing countries in East-West
disputes.

Although political factors usually have been the primary Soviet motivation for expanding economic relations with the developing countries, economic considerations also have been important. While the U.S.S.R. still assigns highest domestic priority to the development of heavy industry, increasing atten- tion is being paid to expanding the availability of agricultural and other consumer goods. Consequently, trade with the developing countries can be advanta- geous to the U.S.S.R. Consumer goods imports from these countries will enable the U.S.S.R. to increase consumption faster than domestic production facili- ties would permit.

A large-scale reorientation of trade toward the U.S.S.R., however, appears unlikely in the near fu- ture as many primary commodities exported by the de- veloping countries still are marginal to Soviet im- port requirements. But such requirements must be viewed in terms of the Soviet Bloc as a whole. The import needs of other Communist countries in Eastern Europe are much more extensive. These countries are important markets for many agricultural raw materials and minerals. As their capability to export indus- trial equipment expands, the natural advantages of trading with the developing countries will become more significant. The acquisition of industrial raw materials and agricultural products from these coun- tries reduces the pressure on the U.S.S.R. to provide these commodities.

Response of the "Neutrals"

But the political character of the Soviet pro- gram was a "two-headed" phenomenon. Political con- siderations also played an important--sometimes pri- mary--part in the decisions of most of the recipients of Soviet economic assistance to accept such aid. The U.S.S.R. found a receptive atmosphere in which to nurture the neutralism which emerged from the Bandung Conference of 1955. The important elements of anti-Western sentiment in many of the former co- lonial territories and the economic aspirations of the developing countries already existed. The U.S.S.R. needed only to present itself as an

additional source of political and economic support
to find a number of willing recipients.

Afghanistan, Egypt, India, and Indonesia read-
ily accepted Soviet assistance. These countries
either sought support for their economic development
programs or for particular political goals. India's
leaders were primarily concerned with obtaining economic assistance from all quarters to further Indian
economic development. Afghanistan and Indonesia were
prompted to accept not only Soviet economic aid for
development purposes, but also political and military
assistance to bolster their stand in regional disputes. Nasser, seeking support against Israel, the
West, and Western-supported institutions in the Middle East, initially accepted Soviet assistance primarily for political and security reasons. Several
other countries quickly accepted large amounts of
Communist economic assistance. Burma, Syria, and
Yemen, displaying "neutralist" policies or seeking
support in regional conflicts, became willing recipients of Soviet economic and military assistance.

These early recipients of Soviet aid generally
were motivated by negative political considerations.
Similar considerations prompted other countries,
particularly in Africa, to accept Communist assistance. But Soviet economic aid subsequently became
respectable in the eyes of many other countries.
The willingness of such countries as Ethiopia, Iran,
Pakistan, and Turkey to accept Soviet economic aid
reflected this development. Although few aid agreements have been concluded with Latin American countries, domestic pressure for economic development
and increasing leftist influence in certain countries have made the prospect of Soviet aid an important consideration in Latin American affairs.

Long-Range Soviet Goals

In the long run, the Soviet objective is to instill a preference for socialist-type institutions
and destroy the economic relations between the industrialized West and the developing countries. The

U.S.S.R. seeks to encourage the growth of the public
sector by channeling its aid toward the state-owned
enterprises. A recurring theme in Communist publica-
tions is that Soviet credits which assist the rapid
development of the state sector are the most important form of economic assistance given to developing
countries by the U.S.S.R.[14] By despatching large
numbers of technicians to recipient countries and
accepting indigenous personnel for academic and technical training in Communist countries, the U.S.S.R.
has exposed many individuals to ideas, techniques,
and institutions known only to a few. At the same
time, it seeks to discredit Western-sponsored institutions and encourages nationalization of foreign-
owned investments. To present itself as an alternative to private investment, the U.S.S.R. must convince recipient countries that its methods offer better prospects for rapid economic development than do
those of the West.

Another long-run Soviet goal is to weaken the
economies of the West by encouraging developing
countries to nationalize foreign private investment.
The expectation is that economic difficulties will
develop in Western economies as a result of the loss
of overseas investments. Furthermore, nationalization, or prospects of nationalization, of private
investment inhibits foreign private investment from
channeling additional capital into these countries.
By encouraging the growth of the state sector, the
U.S.S.R. also seeks to destroy the economic bonds
these countries have with the industrialized West
and to direct their raw materials to the Communist
countries. One author observes:

> By weakening the ties between these
> areas and the Western powers, the So-
> viet Union seeks to achieve a decisive
> leverage effect upon the advanced in-
> dustrial nations, in the expectation
> that the "inevitable" crisis of capi-
> talism will be hastened as markets and
> sources of raw materials are cut off.[15]

This theme is common in Soviet literature. For example, one Soviet spokesman states:

> The growth of economic relations be-
> tween the former colonial countries
> and the socialist countries noticeably
> constricts the sphere of the world cap-
> italist market and expands the sphere
> of activity of the world socialist
> market.[16]

Notes to Chapter 1

1. John H. Ohly, "Competitive Aspects of Foreign Aid," SRI Journal, III (Fourth Quarter, 1959),
178.

2. U.S. Congress, Senate Committee on Foreign
Relations, Foreign Aid, Report of Special Subcommittee to Study the Foreign Aid Program, 85th Cong.,
1st Sess. (Washington: 1957), p. 4.

3. U.S. Congress, Senate Committee on Foreign
Relations, The Objectives of United States Economic
Assistance Programs (Washington: 1957), p. 5.

4. U.S. Department of State, Point 4 (Washington: 1953), p. 3.

5. U.S. Department of Commerce, Foreign Aid by
the United States Government 1940-1951 (Washington:
1952), p. 7.

6. Commission on Foreign Economic Policy, Report to the President and the Congress (Washington:
1954), p. 8.

7. U.S. Congress, Mutual Security Act of 1954,
P.L. 665, 83d Cong., 2d Sess. (Washington: 1954),
p. 6.

8. U.S. Congress, House Committee on Foreign Affairs, Hearings on H.R. 12181, Mutual Security Act of 1958, 85th Cong., 2d Sess. (Washington: 1958), p. 388.

9. Quoted in V. Rymlov, "Economic Competition of the Two Systems and the Problem of Aid to Underdeveloped Countries," Problems of Economics (Moscow), III (December, 1960), 45.

10. U.S. Congress, Senate Committee on Foreign Relations, American Private Enterprise, Foreign Economic Development, and the Aid Program (Washington: 1957), p. XIII.

11. Committee to Strengthen the Security of the Free World, The Scope and Distribution of the United States Military and Economic Assistance Programs (Washington: 1963), p. 19.

12. Milton Kovner, The Challenge of Coexistence (Washington: Public Affairs Press, 1961), p. 52.

13. U.S. Department of State, Communist Economic Policy in the Less Developed Areas (Washington: 1960), p. 6.

14. See, for example, V. Vershinin and V. Demidov, "Disinterested Aid," International Affairs (Moscow), I (January, 1960), 35.

15. Marshall D. Shulman, "The Real Nature of the Soviet Challenge," The New York Times Magazine, July 23, 1961, p. 43.

16. See, for example, G. Kim, Sovremennyi Vostok (Contemporary East), XI (November, 1959), 15.

CHAPTER **2** MAGNITUDE AND
CHARACTER OF
THE AID PROGRAMS

MAGNITUDE AND GEOGRAPHIC DISTRIBUTION

U.S. Economic Aid

By the end of fiscal year 1965, U.S. aid to the
developing countries totaled nearly $44.4 billion.[1]
More than $22.2 billion, or 50 per cent, has been
provided by the Agency for International Development
(AID) and its predecessor agencies. Surplus agricultural commodities sold under the Agricultural
Trade Development Assistance Act of 1954 (P.L. 480)
and loans and long-term credit guarantees by the
Export-Import Bank account for 26 per cent and 12
per cent, respectively. The balance represents aid
provided under a variety of other programs, including postwar relief, the Alliance for Progress, the
Peace Corps, and contributions to international
organizations.

Although the U.S. has provided economic assistance to some ninety developing countries, the bulk
of such aid has been highly concentrated. Nearly
three-fourths of the total has been extended to
sixteen countries. Thirteen recipients of U.S. aid
have received more than $1 billion each and seven
of these countries have been the beneficiaries of
more than $2 billion each. Table 1 presents a list
of the major recipients of U.S. economic assistance.

14

TABLE 1

Major Recipients of U.S. Economic Aid,
FY 1946-FY 1965

(In millions of dollars)

Country	Amount
India	6,318
Korea	4,081
Pakistan	3,035
Brazil	2,622
Viet Nam	2,397
Turkey	2,279
Republic of China	2,273
Greece	1,934
Philippines	1,442
United Arab Republic	1,209
Israel	1,087
Mexico	1,027
Chile	1,026
Indonesia	873
Iran	857
Colombia	666

Source: Agency for International Development,
U.S. Overseas Loans, Grants and Assistance from
International Organizations, July 1, 1945-June 30,
1965 (Washington: 1966).

The types of aid provided, although less concentrated, generally reflect particular regional requirements. Latin American countries have received
69 per cent of the loans authorized by the Export-
Import Bank, indicating the sizable amount of assistance provided to the substantial volume of U.S.
private investment in Latin America. The Far East
has received 38 per cent of total AID obligations,
representing the large sums required to support the
military contributions of South Korea, Viet Nam, and

the Republic of China. South Asia accounts for the
largest share of P.L. 480 assistance, reflecting the
more than $3 billion of surplus agricultural prod-
ucts exported to India. The distribution of the different types of aid is presented in Table 2.

TABLE 2

Types of U.S. Economic Aid to Developing Countries,
FY 1946-FY 1965

(Per cent of total)

	Total Aid	AID	P.L.480	Export-Import Bank	Other
Africa	7	8	8	4	3
Far East	30	38	18	8	56
Latin America	22	13	14	69	21
Middle East	19	21	23	10	13
South Asia	22	20	37	9	7
Total	100	100	100	100	100

Source: Percentages derived from U.S. Overseas
Loans and Grants.

U.S.S.R. Economic Aid

Soviet economic aid totaling more than $5 bil-
lion has been made available to twenty-eight developing countries. From a relatively insignificant
$6 million in 1954, this aid program has grown dra-
matically. Except for a sharp drop in the level of
new aid commitments in 1962, new annual Soviet aid

commitments have been maintained at a relatively
high level. In 1964, Soviet aid extensions totaled
about $1 billion. The geographic distribution of
Soviet economic assistance is highly concentrated;
three countries--Afghanistan, India, and the United
Arab Republic (U.A.R.)--account for 51 per cent of
the total aid extended by the U.S.S.R. The addition
of Algeria, Indonesia, Iran, and Turkey raises the
proportion to 72 per cent.

Although this high degree of concentration
partly reflects initial Soviet efforts to select
strategic target countries as aid recipients, there
is no reason to assume that the U.S.S.R. would not
have concluded agreements with still other countries.
The early recipients were the neutralist countries
which welcomed Soviet aid as an additional source of
capital. Selectivity and receptivity in this con-
text are two sides of the same coin. Such countries
as Afghanistan, India, and the U.A.R. have been recipients of Soviet largesse for nearly a dozen years.
Another factor which has influenced this geographic
concentration has been the ability of these same
countries to absorb large amounts of Soviet aid.

United States economic aid for the comparable
period covered by the Soviet program, i.e., since
mid-1954, has been seven times greater than that of
the U.S.S.R. In certain countries, however, Soviet
commitments are much larger. A comparison of the
magnitude of U.S. and U.S.S.R. economic aid to the
same countries is presented in Table 3.

CHARACTER OF THE U.S. ECONOMIC AID PROGRAM

U.S. economic aid to the developing countries
is provided mainly under several major legislative
authorizations. Grants and loans are provided under
the Foreign Assistance Act of 1961 (as amended);
surplus agricultural commodities through the Agricultural Trade Development and Assistance Act of
1954 (as amended); and loans, credits, and guarantees to finance exports of U.S. goods and services

TABLE 3

U.S. and U.S.S.R. Economic Aid Extended to the Developing Countries,
July, 1945–June, 1965

(In millions of dollars)

| | U.S. Economic Aid | | U.S.S.R. Economic Aid | |
	July, 1945–June, 1965	July, 1954–June, 1965	1954–65 (calendar years)	Per Cent of Total
Total to all developing countries	44,363	35,321	5,030	100.0
Total to selected developing countries	19,446	16,368	5,030	100.0
Afghanistan	305	281	552	10.9
Algeria	162	162	230	4.6
Argentina	651	452	115	2.3
Burma	121	95	14	*
Cambodia	256	256	21	*
Ceylon	98	98	30	*
Congo (Brazzaville)	2	2	9	*
Ethiopia	151	151	102	2.0
Ghana	165	164	89	1.8
Greece	1,934	572	84	1.7

Guinea	77	77	70	1.4
India	6,318	5,901	1,022	20.3
Indonesia	873	580	372	7.4
Iran	857	703	330	6.6
Iraq	53	52	184	3.6
Kenya	36	32	44	0.9
Mali	14	14	55	1.1
Nepal	85	84	20	*
Pakistan	3,035	2,891	94	1.9
Senegal	18	18	7	*
Somali Republic	47	47	57	1.1
Sudan	97	97	22	*
Syrian Arab Republic	91	90	150	2.9
Tunisia	456	456	28	*
Turkey	2,279	1,873	210	4.2
Uganda	17	17	16	*
United Arab Republic	1,209	1,173	1,011	20.1
Yemen	39	39	92	1.8

*Less than 0.5 per cent.

Source: U.S. Overseas Loans and Grants; U.S. Department of State, Research Memorandum, RSB-65, "The Communist Economic Offensive Through 1964," August 4, 1965 (mimeographed); Middle East Economic Digest, January 21, 1966; New York Times, February 25, 1965; November 13, 1965.

under the Export-Import Bank Act of 1945 (as amended).
The Alliance for Progress provides an additional
source of aid for Latin American countries.

Agency for International Development

The U.S. has provided assistance to developing
countries totaling $22.3 billion under the Foreign
Assistance Act of 1961 and preceding programs. U.S.
assistance currently is being dispensed through the
Agency for International Development (AID).[2] The
bulk of this aid has been in the form of supporting
assistance, labeled defense support prior to fiscal
year 1962. The primary method of disbursing AID
assistance is by nonproject expenditures to finance
imports of agricultural or industrial commodities.
U.S. funds are paid to the suppliers of materials or
services delivered to the recipient country.

The proportion of total aid requests represented
by supporting assistance has varied with the changing demands placed upon the aid program. The Administration's request for $1.3 billion for defense
support constituted 23 per cent of total Mutual Security Program appropriations for fiscal year 1957.[3]
The obligations under this category in fiscal year
1961 declined to $724 million but accounted for 32
per cent of total AID obligations. During fiscal
year 1964, supporting assistance dropped to about
$360 million but jumped sharply in fiscal year 1965
as the amount allocated for Viet Nam nearly doubled.
Since 1961, such assistance has been highly concentrated, with the bulk allocated to countries along
the periphery of the Communist world.

It is difficult to determine the extent to which
outlays under supporting assistance have constituted
a net addition to the resources of a recipient country. Its emphasis on support for a country's military contribution affects its value for economic development. Combined with military outlays, such expenditures may even have inflationary effects if the
country's economy cannot absorb such assistance.
Moreover, the diversion of resources and manpower to

military and defense supporting activities hampers
over-all economic development.

During the latter years of the second Eisen-
hower Administration (1957-61), the idea of long-
term aid for economic development gained acceptance
and emphasis shifted from grant aid to loans repayable mainly in local currencies. This change was
reflected in the Draper Committee report, which en-
dorsed economic aid in the following words:

> The substantial expenditures made by
> our Government in recent years for
> economic assistance are justified on
> grounds both of enlightened self-
> interest and of our moral responsi-
> bility to ourselves to do what we can
> to help other peoples realize their
> legitimate aspirations.[4]

The organization established under the Mutual
Security Act of 1957 to administer this part of the
aid program was the Development Loan Fund (DLF).
The stated objective of the DLF was to assist in
initiating economic improvements in aid-receiving
countries as a prelude to later investment:

> Basic developmental activities fre-
> quently carried on by governments
> (such as power, transportation, com-
> munication facilities, irrigation,
> reclamation and drainage projects,
> certain educational projects) are
> eligible for financing by the Devel-
> opment Loan Fund. Proposals for such
> financing must show that the project
> will make a clear contribution to the
> long-range economic development and
> growth of the country concerned. Par-
> ticularly favored will be those ac-
> tivities which lay a base for, or
> eventually make possible, productive
> private investment. Joint ventures
> between private American investors and

private investors from abroad, including investors from third countries
will be looked upon with favor.[5]

Originally established as an autonomous organization, the DLF was absorbed by AID in November,
1961. The DLF now functions as AID's disburser of
economic development loan funds. Since mid-1957,
authorizations for such loans have totaled $5.1 bil-
lion, of which $3.1 billion had been expended by
mid-1965. Three countries--India, Pakistan, and
Turkey--received 68 per cent of total loan authorizations.

Another important component of AID's program is
the provision of technical assistance. Such aid has
been available to the developing countries since
May, 1950. The technical assistance program is es-
sentially a program for the exchange of technical
knowledge and skills designed "to contribute primarily to the balanced and integrated development of
the economic resources and productive capacities of
economically underdeveloped areas."[6] By the end of
fiscal year 1965, about $2 billion had been obli-
gated for technical assistance programs in developing countries.

The technical assistance program generally is
designed to effect a transfer of skills to increase
production and productivity. In carrying out these
programs, AID draws on the specialized knowledge,
skills, and experience of American universities, industry, voluntary agencies, and other U.S. Government agencies. It sends specialists abroad to help
train local technicians, and it brings individuals
from developing countries to the U.S. for advanced
study or observation of agricultural, industrial,
and administrative techniques. Most technical assistance programs generally emphasize the funda-
mentals of agriculture, health, and education.
Other important categories include community development, public administration, industry, and mining.

U.S. technical assistance generally is provided
without charge to the recipient country. The cost

of technical services and project equipment is provided as a grant-in-aid. Host country contributions
usually include land for demonstration farms, buildings for health clinics, vocational schools, and
other similar facilities. Salaries of local employees are paid by the host government which also provides transportation for U.S. supplies and equipment
used within the country.

The Agricultural Trade Development
and Assistance Act

Since the early 1950's, the rising stocks of
surplus agricultural commodities accumulated under
domestic price-support programs have become an increasingly important form of foreign aid. Although
some commodities were available to aid recipients
under earlier foreign aid legislation, the first major program of this type was initiated under Section
550 of the Mutual Security Act of 1953, authorizing
sales for local currencies. This authorization was
continued in Section 402 of the Mutual Security Act
of 1954. The latter act required that specified
portions of foreign aid appropriations be used for
the purchase of surplus agricultural commodities
which could be sold abroad for foreign currencies.
More important than either of these acts, however,
is the Agricultural Trade Development and Assistance
Act of 1954 (P.L. 480), which permits the sale of
surplus commodities for local currencies and the
lending or granting of these currencies for military
and economic aid purposes. Since the enactment of
P.L. 480, assistance totaling nearly $11.9 billion
had been provided to developing countries by the end
of June, 1965. India is by far the major recipient
of such aid, having concluded agreements totaling
$3.1 billion.

P.L. 480 provides for the disposal of agricultural surplus commodities in several ways:

1. Under Title I, they can be sold for foreign
currencies.

2. Under Title II, they can be used to furnish

famine relief and other emergency assistance.

3. Under Title III, they can be donated to
nonprofit voluntary bodies for assistance to individuals outside the U.S.

4. Under Title IV, they can be sold for dollars
under long-term credit agreements between foreign
governments and U.S. and foreign private trade en-
tities.[7]

The foreign currencies obtained from the sale
of agricultural commodities in foreign markets can
be used for three major purposes:

1. Loans and grants for economic development
and grants for military purposes;

2. loans to private American and, in certain
cases, foreign enterprises; and

3. administrative expenses of the U.S. Government at posts in recipient countries, marketing programs, exchange programs, and other similar purposes.

Although the sale of surplus agricultural commodities plays an important part in the foreign aid
program, an important consideration originally underlying the disposal of these commodities was the desire to dispose of the rapidly mounting stocks of
agricultural commodities and "to increase the consumption of United States agricultural commodities
in foreign countries."[8]

Export-Import Bank

The Export-Import Bank is an important source
of medium- and long-term loans to purchase capital
goods, raw materials, and technical services. The
Export-Import Bank was established in 1934 to pro-
mote U.S. foreign trade but currently operates under
the Export-Import Bank Act of 1945, as amended. The
Bank fosters U.S. trade by extending dollar loans,
providing guarantees on dollar loans made by other

institutions, and administering loans extended by
other government agencies. The main purpose of the
Bank is to "assist, support, and encourage" the overseas trade of U.S. private enterprise. All of the
"operations of the Bank are related to this primary
purpose."[9] In pursuing this objective, the Bank is
guided by the principle that all its dollar loans
must offer a reasonable assurance of repayment in
U.S. dollars. Between the end of World War II and
June 30, 1965, the Bank had authorized medium- and
long-term loans to the developing countries totaling
$5.2 billion. Latin American countries received 69
per cent of these authorizations. Brazil, Mexico,
and Argentina received two-thirds of total authorizations for that region.

The Export-Import Bank finances a wide variety
of projects and commodities. Table 4 presents a list
of items financed in fiscal year 1960 and serves as
an example of the types of projects accepted by the
Bank.

The Bank also administers some of the foreign
currencies under Section 104 (a) of P.L. 480, the
section known as the Cooley Amendment. Up to 25 per
cent of the currencies arising from the sale of surplus agricultural commodities abroad may be used for
loans to business firms in the countries concerned.
These loans may be made either to U.S. firms and af-
filiates for the expansion of trade or to local
firms setting up facilities which will in turn increase the markets for U.S. agricultural surpluses.

Alliance for Progress

Since mid-1962, the U.S. has been providing
economic assistance to Latin American countries under the Alliance for Progress. Although launched
under the late President Kennedy in a speech delivered on March 13, 1961, the program stems largely
from the Act of Bogota proclaimed on September 12,
1960. The act pledged the Latin American nations to
join in solving mutual social and economic problems.
The broad objectives of Bogota subsequently were

TABLE 4

Export Items Financed by the Export-Import Bank
in Fiscal Year 1960

(In millions of dollars)

Item	Amount
Electric power equipment	95.9
Aircraft and airport equipment	94.9
Raw cotton	70.0
Fertilizer plant equipment	50.8
Railroad equipment	36.9
Trade emergencies	30.0
Steel mill equipment	28.2
Agricultural production and processing equipment	26.5
Harbor development	22.7
Automotive industry equipment	18.3
Hotel construction	18.1
Nonferrous metal production	15.8
Textile mill equipment	14.1
Mining development	11.2
Rehabilitation	10.0
Telecommunications equipment	9.2
Highway construction	5.6
Miscellaneous	25.9
Total	584.1

Source: Export-Import Bank of Washington,
Report to the Congress for the Twelve Months Ending
June 30, 1960 (Washington: 1960), p. v.

translated into specific targets at a meeting of
ministerial representatives of the American states
at Punta del Este in August, 1961. The participating countries approved the concept of an Alliance
for Progress and declared:

> The Alliance is established on the
> basic principle that free men working
> through institutions of representative
> democracy can best satisfy man's aspi-
> rations, including those for work, home
> and land, health and schools.[10]

The American states pledged at least $100 bil-
lion in ten years toward achieving these goals.
During the first three years of the program, the
U.S. obligated $496 million under the Social Prog-
ress Trust Fund administered by the Inter-American
Development Bank and $1.4 billion in loans through
AID.

CHARACTER OF SOVIET ECONOMIC AID

The Credit Agreement

Most Soviet economic assistance is dispensed
within the framework of long-term, interest-bearing
credits. Of the total aid extended by the end of
1965, only $156 million represents grant aid. Usu-
ally a financial aid agreement provides a line of
credit to be used for specific projects subsequently agreed upon. Occasionally, a major agreement is
concluded for a specific project, e.g., the Bhilai
steel mill in India or the Aswan Dam in the U.A.R.
The financial aid under the Soviet credit generally
is available for a specified number of years. Only
after the recipient country has agreed to accept a
credit is its specific allocation determined and
technical surveys undertaken. Consequently, substantial drawings on a credit may not take place
until a few years after its extension. The credits
extended to India in 1959, for example, were for use
during the third five-year plan which began in April,
1961.

Generally, Soviet credits are available for the purchase of machinery, equipment, and materials for specific projects to be constructed under the credit. The cost of the services of Soviet technical personnel employed in all phases of construction of a project is also included under the credit agreement. Many agreements cover the cost of training in the U.S.S.R. indigenous technical personnel who eventually will be employed on the project to be constructed. The local costs incurred by Soviet personnel during employment in the recipient country are borne by the host country and are not chargeable to the credit.

Although Soviet assistance provides the financing for the foreign-exchange component of a construction project, the use of such aid often is delayed by the recipient's inability to provide the local currency portion of the total cost of the project. Economic aid from the U.S.S.R. rarely is expended to cover the local costs of Soviet-financed projects. As far as is known, there is only one country where sizable amounts of commodities were imported for sale in the domestic market to generate local currency. Part of the Soviet credit of $100 million to Afghanistan was used to import consumer goods to generate local currency to cover the domestic costs of a multipurpose project. The proceeds from the sale of 40,000 tons of Soviet wheat granted to Afghanistan in 1959 also were available for construction of the Kushka-Kandahar highway.[11]

Types of Projects

The type of assistance provided by the U.S.S.R. often is criticized for its emphasis on "impact-type" projects and for its concentration on industry. One cannot be certain as to what is meant by an "impact-type" project. Presumably it refers to any project which can be completed rapidly and leaves a profound impression on the local population. Among the examples of this technique often cited are a bakery complex and paved street in Kabul, a hotel in Burma, and the Asian Games stadium in Indonesia. But these projects are relatively

few. The bulk of Soviet assistance actually is being channeled into basic industrial facilities and
overhead investment.

The initial "impact" of Soviet aid agreements
often has been of a political character. This is
particularly true at a time when the recipient country seeks to taunt a Western power with which its
political relations have been strained. The initial
economic aid agreements with Egypt, Syria, and Indonesia, for example, occurred during periods of in-
tense nationalistic disturbances. Certainly the
willingness of the Soviet Union to construct the
Aswan Dam had a profound psychological impact on the
Egyptians after Western refusal to undertake the
project.

The observation that Soviet assistance is concentrated in industry is only partially correct. It
is true that from the Soviet viewpoint, the development of industry is an important aspect of its aid
program. Through this device the U.S.S.R. seeks to
preempt private capital in industry by performing
the same function. Communist doctrine holds that a
developing country is not truly independent unless
it develops and owns its industrial sector. But in
most of these countries industry plays only a small
part in the total of economic activity. Consequently, the amount of assistance which the U.S.S.R. can
provide for the industrial sector must be limited.

Although Soviet spokesmen frequently emphasize
the need for the development of industry in developing countries, they have not neglected other economic sectors. Speaking before the delegates to the
Afro-Asian Conference in Cairo on December 27, 1957,
the chief Soviet representative stated:

> The development of various branches of
> the manufacturing industry cannot be
> effected otherwise than by expanding
> agriculture and the extracting indus-
> try. . . . It should be noted that
> agriculture and the extracting industry

> may become the basis for developing
> many other branches of the economy and
> a source of foreign exchange. . . .[12]

The financing of such an ambitious undertaking could,
he indicated, be accomplished by nationalizing industry and trade.

About half of Soviet aid has been allocated for
industrial expansion and nearly 35 per cent for the
construction of hydroelectric, irrigation, and
transportation facilities. The proportion accounted
for by industry is much smaller if aid to India--the
recipient of 40 per cent of Soviet assistance for
industry--is subtracted. In almost every other
country receiving aid from the U.S.S.R., major multipurpose and transportation projects are to be undertaken. Such projects eventually will account for
the largest share of Soviet economic assistance to
Afghanistan, Ceylon, Guinea, Iraq, Indonesia, Syria,
and Yemen. These projects not only are not impact
projects but will require from five to ten years to
complete. The U.S.S.R. also is engaged in a variety
of other undertakings. Development of mineral resources, particularly petroleum, forms an important
part of the Soviet aid program. Important mineral
development programs have been undertaken or are in
progress in Afghanistan, Ghana, Guinea, India, Indonesia, Syria, and the U.A.R.

Although of lesser importance in the Soviet program, assistance is being provided for municipal and
public utilities, public health, medicine, and tour-
ism. Water and sewage systems, small electric power
plants for rural areas, housing developments, and
local transportation facilities are being constructed
in a number of countries. Hospitals were built in
Burma, Cambodia, Guinea, and Nepal. Assistance for
the construction of hotels in Burma and Ghana and
sports stadiums in Guinea and Indonesia also form
part of the Soviet aid program. The latter projects
undoubtedly could be replaced with others of a higher economic priority.

Technical Assistance

An important aspect of the Soviet program is the provision of technical assistance. The bulk of such assistance is paid for by the recipient and usually is dispensed within the framework of the credit agreement. The type of assistance provided resembles, in large part, the non-aid technical services of Western private firms in connection with construction contracts and the sale of industrial equipment.

The number of Soviet technicians sent to recipient countries has increased rapidly since the inception of the U.S.S.R.'s aid program. During the latter half of 1957, 1,110 technicians were employed on projects in developing countries.[13] During 1963, the number had increased nearly eightfold, rising to 8,625.[14] The functions in which these technicians usually are engaged range from operation of heavy construction equipment to advising on economic planning. Most of these technicians, however, are connected with specific projects under the credit agreements.

The number of students and technical trainees sent to the U.S.S.R. for training has increased even more dramatically. In 1957, more than 2,000 nationals from developing countries received training in the U.S.S.R.[15] By the end of 1964, the number had risen to about 11,900.[16] Almost all academic students attend Soviet universities on scholarships usually arranged within the framework of government-to-government cultural agreements. Technical trainees generally are sent to the U.S.S.R. to be trained for positions they will fill when a Soviet project in the recipient country is completed. For example, nearly 700 Indian engineers and skilled workers employed at Bhilai were trained at Soviet steel plants.[17]

By sending large numbers of Soviet technicians to the developing countries and accepting their nationals for study and training, the U.S.S.R. is exposing recipients of its aid to its techniques and

methods of operations. That the Communists consider
this important is reflected by an article in a Soviet publication:

> The world system of Socialism exercises
> the widest and most direct influence on
> all aspects of the development of the
> State-capitalist sector of the indepen-
> dent countries of the East, not only by
> means of direct economic support but
> also by the popularity of its methods
> and forms of economic construction.[18]

COMPARATIVE REPAYMENT TERMS

Loans and credits extended by the U.S. under
the economic aid program and by the Export-Import
Bank have had varying repayment terms. Prior to
1954, economic aid loans generally were to be repaid in U.S. dollars. The Mutual Security Act of
1954 permitted the option of repayment in dollars
or local currency. This option reflected the growing consideration for a recipient's future ability
to repay the loan and subsequently was incorporated
into the repayment terms on DLF loans. The length
of repayment for former MSP loans is between 10-40
years and for DLF loans, 3-40 years. All loans
generally provide a grace period of 1-7 years. Interest on these loans ranges from 3 to 5-3/4 per
cent. Loans repaid in local currency carry a larger
interest charge.

The Foreign Assistance Act of 1961 requires all
AID loans to be repaid in dollars. The length of
repayment, however, was set at 40 years with a ten-
year grace period and interest charges at 0.75
per cent. The average terms of repayment of loans
from the Export-Import Bank have been about seven
years.[19] The bank makes no loans for periods of
less than a year nor more than 25 years. In recent
years, the interest rates charged by the bank for
loans to foreign governments and loans with government guarantees has averaged 5 to $5\frac{1}{2}$ per cent.

Credits extended by the U.S.S.R. usually require repayment over a period of 12 years beginning
one year after delivery of all equipment for the
project for which the credit was provided. There
are some rare exceptions, e.g., the $100 million
credit to Afghanistan extended in 1955, which is to
be repaid in 22 years after an eight-year grace
period. The usual repayment clause contained in
Soviet credits stipulates that repayment is to be
made in commodities or convertible currency. The
meaning of this clause is not clear. If the debtor
country is required to repay in convertible currency, a major incentive for accepting Soviet assistance disappears. It seems likely that the U.S.S.R.
will insist upon convertible currency only when adequate supplies of goods are not available.

Repayment of Soviet credits with commodities
generally is considered to be a major step in solving the problem of export surpluses in recipient
countries. It is also assumed that such repayment
will result in substantial increases in trade between the U.S.S.R. and recipient countries.[20] This
benefit is more apparent than real as the relative
amounts involved actually will be only a small portion of the total trade of these countries. For
example, repayment of the $258 million worth of So-
viet credits extended to India during the years
1955-57 was scheduled to reach a peak of about $25
million in 1965. Repayments of all Soviet credits
extended to Indonesia and the U.A.R. prior to 1964
are expected to reach peaks of $30 million and $45
million in 1967 and 1968, respectively. These repayments amount to 2 per cent, 3 per cent, and 8 per
cent, respectively, of Indian, Indonesian, and U.A.R.
exports in 1960. Even if repayment of other Bloc
credits is included, the percentages will not
change significantly. They might even decline if
it is assumed that the exports of the developing
countries will rise substantially during the next
five years. Although these relatively small sums
are not unimportant, the major benefit to the developing country is that it will not have to draw further on its meager foreign-exchange reserves.

One of the features of Soviet credits which ap-
peals to developing countries is the relatively low
interest charge of 2.5 per cent. This rate has not
changed over time. On major credits, the lower interest rates yield substantial savings. The Indian
Government, for example, estimated that the difference between the interest charged for construction
of the Bhilai steel mill and that charged for the
German-built Rourekala plant was expected to result
in a saving of about $17 million, equal to about 10
per cent of the German credit for the plant.[21] The
real savings from lower interest rates, however, depend on the value received. It is difficult to assess the real value of a steel mill which cannot be
sold on the world market.

Notes to Chapter 2

1. The total of U.S. economic aid does not include local currencies which have accrued to the U.S.
as counterpart funds or from sales of agricultural
commodities in the markets of recipient countries
and subsequently are loaned or granted to the host
government.

2. The predecessors of AID were the Foreign
Operations Administration, the Mutual Security Administration, the Economic Cooperation Administration, and the International Cooperation Administration.

3. U.S. Department of State, The Mutual Security Program, Fiscal Year 1957 (Washington: 1956),
p. 11.

4. Composite Report of the President's Committee to Study the United States Military Assistance
Program, I (Washington: 1959), 60.

5. The Development Loan Fund (Washington:
1957), p. 1.

6. U.S. Senate, Committee on Foreign Relations, Technical Assistance, 85th Cong., 1st Sess. (Washington: 1957), p. 91.

7. Public Law 480, Agricultural Trade Development and Assistance Act of 1954, 83d Cong. (Washington: 1954).

8. Ibid., p. 1.

9. Export-Import Bank of Washington, General Policies (Washington: 1959), p. 1.

10. Pan American Union, "Declaration to the Peoples of America," Alliance for Progress (Washington: 1961), p. 3.

11. Peter G. Frank, Afghanistan between East and West (Washington: National Planning Association, 1960), p. 58.

12. Quoted in Current Digest of the Soviet Press, February 5, 1958, pp. 25-26.

13. Waldemar A. Nielsen and Zoran S. Hodjera, "Sino-Soviet Bloc Technical Assistance--Another Bilateral Approach," The Annals, CCCXXIII (May, 1959), 41.

14. U.S. Department of State, Research Memorandum, RSB-43, "The Communist Economic Offensive through 1963," June 18, 1964. (Mimeographed.)

15. Michael Sapir, The New Role of the Soviets in the World Economy (New York: Committee for Economic Development, 1958), p. 18.

16. U.S. Department of State, Research Memorandum, RSB-49, "Educational and Cultural Exchange between Communist Countries and the Free World in 1964," June 1, 1965. (Mimeographed.)

17. The New York Times, May 22, 1960, p. 4.

18. Kim, op. cit., p. 14.

19. Marjorie W. Hald, The Export-Import Bank and Development Lending (Santa Monica: The Rand Corporation, 1959), p. 19.

20. See, for example, U.S. Congress, Joint Economic Committee, Comparisons of the United States and Soviet Economies, Papers Submitted to Subcommittee on Economic Statistics, 86th Cong., 1st Sess. (Washington: 1959), p. 451.

21. The Eastern Economist, February 11, 1955, p. 218.

CHAPTER **3** TURKEY: EMPHASIS
ON U.S. ECONOMIC
ASSISTANCE

The political and economic problems confronting
many of the developing countries today find their
parallel in those experienced in Turkey in the early
days of the Republic. Fired by an uncompromising
nationalism, racked by the turmoil of sudden social
and political change, deficient in capital, and suspicious of foreign investment, Turkish leaders,
nevertheless, were determined to embark on a policy
of rapid economic development. Economic development
was inseparable from Westernization--to the Turks,
the symbol of political and social development. But
the major economic choice Turkey faced in the early
1920's is the one facing many developing countries
today: Shall the state or private enterprise have
primary responsibility for spurring the drive for
economic development and industrialization?

HISTORICAL BACKGROUND

During the early years of the Ataturk Government, the lack of capital, organizational ability,
and entrepreneurial and technical skills prompted
the regime to rely largely on domestic private enterprise. In 1924, the Ish Bank was established
with the responsibility for providing capital to
encourage private enterprise in the industrial sector. Legislation enacted in 1927 was designed to
encourage investment in industry by granting to industrial firms government-owned land, buildings, and
other facilities.[1]

In spite of these measures, Turkish industrial
expansion during the 1920's fell far short of the

Turkish leaders' expectations. This disappointment
became more pronounced with the onset of the depression of the 1930's and the subsequent decline in export earnings. Throughout this period government
efforts to initiate a desired rate of growth also
were hampered by limited domestic financial resources. The low level of income prevented adequate
private capital accumulation and the generally low
level of consumption limited the extent to which increased austerity measures could secure additional
savings for investment purposes. The Turkish leaders subsequently turned to the development of a system of government-owned industrial enterprises established with public funds--a program they termed
etatism.

In 1933, the Sumerbank was created with the responsibility for establishing, financing, and manag-
ing industrial enterprises. In 1934, influenced by
the trend toward centralized economic direction in
Europe, Turkey embarked on a five-year development
program designed to industrialize the Turkish economy. Its aim was twofold: to increase the production and eliminate the importation of consumer goods
and to establish basic primary industries on which
secondary industries subsequently could be based.
The U.S.S.R. provided Turkey with the idea of, and
some capital for, a state-controlled, planned, industrial expansion. A Soviet credit of $8 million
enabled Turkey to begin expanding its system of
state enterprises, particularly in textile production.[2] But in spite of the growth of the state enterprise system, Turkey never accepted etatism as a
political doctrine. The concept was not identified
with socialism but, rather, it was viewed as a prag-
matic intermingling of state and private enterprise
with the state providing the necessary infrastructure and filling other gaps in investment. The
Ataturk Regime looked upon the state enterprise system as a temporary phase which would be abandoned as
soon as the private sector could assume the leading
role in Turkey's economic development.[3]

The economic policy of etatism prevailed offi-
cially into the late 1940's. By that time new

political and economic forces emerged in the opposition parties which pressed for an adjustment in economic policy to the more liberal Western standards.
The prospect of large-scale foreign, particularly
U.S., economic assistance was an important factor in
this development. These pressures compelled the
Turkish Government to consider halting further expansion of the state enterprises. Moreover, private
capital was to be permitted to play a more active
role in Turkey's economic development. Private participation would be circumscribed only in those
fields where the regime considered state ownership
necessary, e.g., in the fields of transportation and
communication, coal production, and public utilities.[4] In 1950, the Democratic Party, expounding a
policy of economic liberalism and committed to the
dismantling of the state enterprise system, was
elected into power. The new government did not
abandon plans for rapid economic development or industrialization. It did, however, assign a large
role to the private sector and actively sought
large-scale foreign economic assistance. Moreover,
greater attention was to be paid to the development
of agriculture as the most important source of capital for over-all economic development.

ECONOMIC DEVELOPMENT IN TURKEY

Economic development in Turkey since 1950 must
be divided into two major periods. The first period,
representing the years of the Menderes Regime of the
1950's, was characterized by rapid growth, inflation,
uncoordinated development, and almost unlimited sums
of foreign economic assistance and borrowing. The
second period, beginning in 1960, followed the oust-
er of Menderes and witnessed Turkish efforts to
grapple with the country's pressing financial problems, to institute some form of planned development,
and to use its external assistance more effectively.

Growth of the National Product, 1950-60

The Turkish economy expanded rapidly during the
1950's. The area under cultivation doubled, electric

power production increased fourfold, communications
and transportation facilities were expanded substantially, and sizable increases were registered in
manufacturing and mineral production. In terms of
1948 prices, gross national product (GNP) increased
at an average annual rate of 6.4 per cent. This
growth figure, however, obscures two essential facts:
(1) a short period of rapid growth followed by a
longer period of a declining rate of growth; and
(2) the extent to which the rate of economic growth
is dependent upon the vicissitudes of the agricultural sector.

Between 1950 and 1953, the Turkish economy experienced a significant rate of real growth, increasing at an average of 11.8 per cent annually.
In 1954, this trend received a sharp setback because
of an extremely poor harvest; GNP actually declined
9.2 per cent. Over-all economic expansion was re-
sumed in 1955, but it never regained its original
momentum. After 1953, the economy grew at an average annual rate of 4.1 per cent, in spite of significant increases in the four-year period of 1955-58.
An 11.8 per cent increase registered in 1958 resulted
from a 17.5 per cent jump in agricultural production
during that year. The annual increases in GNP are
presented in Table 5.

As indicated above, the inability of the Turkish
economy to regain the high rate of growth achieved
between 1950 and 1953 was, for the most part, the result of stagnation in the agricultural sector. Periodic droughts considerably affected the level of
agricultural production. Moreover, agricultural
production in general did not expand sufficiently to
meet Turkish domestic and export requirements. This
combination of factors tended to affect Turkey's
balance-of-payments adversely and depleted its
foreign-exchange reserves. These difficulties in
Turkey's external accounts, combined with the growing
unwillingness of foreign suppliers to provide short-
term commercial credits, necessitated periodic cur-
tailment of essential imports which, in turn, slowed
the rate of growth in other sectors of the economy.

TABLE 5

Growth of Turkish Gross National Product,*
1950-60

(In billions of lira)

	Gross National Product	Annual Percentage Increase
1950	10.4	
1952	13.0	
1953	14.5	11.1
1954	13.1	-9.2
1955	14.2	7.6
1956	15.1	6.8
1957	16.1	6.3
1958	17.9	11.8
1959	18.7	4.3
1960	19.3	3.2

*At 1948 prices.

Source: AID, "Turkish Economic Statistics"
(Ankara: USOM Turkey, 1962), p. 8. (Mimeographed.)

The declining rate of economic growth takes on greater significance when viewed in terms of individual income. Although real per capita income increased 39.2 per cent between 1950 and 1960, the major share of this increase occurred during the first three years of that period. During those ten years, population increased at an average annual rate of 2.9 per cent and per capita income at 3.3 per cent. This growth in population and per capita income is presented in Table 6.

TABLE 6

Growth of Population and Trend of Per Capita
National Income in Turkey,
1950-60

	Population (In thousands)	Per Capita Income (In Turkish lira at 1948 prices)
1950	20,947	434
1953	22,818	634
1955	24,065	555
1956	24,771	539
1957	25,498	549
1958	26,247	597
1959	27,017	604
1960	27,810	604

Source: Republic of Turkey, National Income of Turkey 1948-1959 (Ankara: Central Statistical Office, 1960), p. 5; National Income of Turkey 1953-1960 (1961), p. 5.

Large-scale efforts to develop the agricultural sector were not undertaken until 1950. By 1953, almost 15 million additional acres of land had been brought under cultivation while agricultural production almost doubled.[5]   Cereal production,

particularly wheat, the export of which was to be a
major source of finance for Turkey's economic development, received particular emphasis. Between 1950
and 1953, acreage devoted to grain production increased about 45 per cent and output doubled, especially the production of wheat and barley. The production of other major crops, e.g., cotton and sugar
beets, also expanded rapidly.

But a severe drought in 1954 halted the rapid
expansion of agricultural production. Between 1953
and 1960, the production of cereals increased only
6 per cent. Concomitantly, the share of the agricultural sector in the national income of Turkey experienced a declining trend after 1953. During the
four-year period of most rapid growth, agriculture
accounted for more than half of Turkey's national
income after that time. In 1960, agriculture's
share fell to 43.9 per cent.

In addition to the impact of climatic conditions, Turkish agriculture also is affected by the
need to utilize sizable amounts of marginal acreage.
It has been estimated that the acreage which can be
ploughed without danger of serious erosion totals
only 30.5 million acres. In 1956, however, the area
under cultivation totaled 55.3 million acres.[6] Moreover, a large part of the crop area lies fallow each
year. Land actually under cultivation accounted for
68 per cent of the total arable land in 1957.

Expansion of production in the industrial sector generally followed a pattern similar to that of
agriculture. Except for a few protected industries,
the growth of industrial production after 1953 was
relatively small, despite substantial public and
private investment in manufacturing enterprises.
Between 1950 and 1953, the production of iron and
steel rose 87 per cent, cement 28 per cent, sugar
32 per cent, and cotton and wool manufactures by lesser amounts. Production of coal, chrome ore, and
iron ore increased 30 per cent, 116 per cent, and
113 per cent, respectively. The large increases in
the production of iron and steel and chrome and iron

ores reflect the small base from which these industries developed.

Following the setback experienced by the Turkish economy in 1954, the rate of growth of industrial output slackened considerably. Inflationary
pressures which had been building slowly since 1951
began to gather momentum. As domestic production
declined, prices increased rapidly. Exports declined
and serious balance-of-payments difficulties and
shortages of foreign exchange developed. Consequently, the demand stimulated by the development program
no longer could be channeled toward imports. Imports of raw materials and spare parts for machinery
also were curtailed and, in turn, affected the level
of industrial production. On the average, imported
goods and materials accounted for about 30 per cent
of total industrial investment in Turkey.[7] As a result, the industrial sector's contribution to Turkey's national income remained relatively constant
during the decade ending in 1960: about 11 per cent.

An increase of 10 per cent was registered in
the contribution of the other sectors to total national income, mainly in those sectors rendering
services. The transportation and electric power
sectors experienced a large measure of growth as a
result of the government's emphasis on the development of social overhead facilities.

PATTERN OF INVESTMENT

Gross Domestic Investment

With the initiation of large-scale development
expenditures in Turkey, the aggregate level of investment increased rapidly. Between 1950 and 1954,
gross investment more than doubled, rising from
about TL 1 billion to TL 2.1 billion. In 1959, the
level of gross investment reached TL 3.1 billion.
The rate of increase, however, did not keep pace
with the growth of the national product. The trend
of the ratio of gross investment to GNP is presented
in Table 7.

TABLE 7

Gross Investment in Turkey,*
1950-60

	Gross Investment (billion TL)	As a Percentage of Gross National Product
1950	1.0	9.6
1951	1.2	11.2
1952	1.7	13.1
1953	1.9	13.1
1954	2.1	16.0
1955	2.3	16.2
1956	2.2	14.6
1957	2.1	13.0
1958	2.6	14.5
1959	3.1	16.6
1960	3.1	16.1

*At 1948 prices.

Source: OEEC, Turkey 1958, EC(59)10 (Paris: 1959), p. 13; The Union of Chambers of Commerce, Industry and Commodity Exchange of Turkey, Economic Report 1962 (Ankara: 1962), p. 13.

The Public Sector

In spite of the Democratic Party's proclaimed intention of reducing the extent of its direct participation in Turkish economic activity, the economic policies and activities of the central government

continued to affect the rate of economic growth in
individual sectors. Investment financed with funds
allocated directly from the budget and from the revenue of government-controlled enterprises continued
to exert an important influence on the pattern of
aggregate investment. Government assistance in the
form of tax exemptions, subsidies, and the provision
of credit facilities also affected the size of investment in certain sectors. When the effects of
these factors are considered along with those re-
sulting from the priority granted the state-owned
enterprises in the allocation of resources, import
licenses, labor, and raw materials, the influence of
government activities on investment obviously has
been very large.

In 1950, the Election Manifesto of the Democratic Party stated:

> To accelerate the development of pri-
> vate enterprise and increase the na-
> tional wealth, it is necessary to put
> a definite stop to a policy whereby
> national resources are . . . wasted by
> the state in non-productive fields of
> activity.[8]

The newly elected Democratic Party, dedicated
to a policy of rapid economic development and spurred
on by the prospect of foreign aid, initiated large-
scale plans for industrial development. The government announced its policy of encouraging private enterprise to participate in Turkey's industrial development and offered to sell the state-owned industries
to private interests. But except for the sale of a
small number of shipping, airline, and petroleum
holdings to private companies, no concerted effort
was made to dispose of the state enterprises. The
government not only failed to dispose of its holdings in a number of major industries originally
scheduled for denationalization (particularly cotton
and woolen textiles, brick and tile, and cement), but
substantially increased its investments in these
same industries.

In spite of the government's unwillingness, or
inability, to dispose of its business assets, its
favorable attitude toward private investment enabled
this sector to expand at a faster rate than the
state enterprises. Whereas in 1949 the private
sector accounted for 50.4 per cent of total industrial investment and 70.2 per cent of industrial capacity, by 1957 the private sector's share of total
industrial investment and industrial capacity had
risen to 64.3 per cent and 84.4 per cent, respectively.

But in 1958, this trend was reversed. The
shortage of foreign exchange and difficulties in ar-
ranging short-term commercial credits with foreign
suppliers resulted in a decline in the level of imports. Expansion of industrial production was affected seriously as imports of industrial raw materials and spare parts were curtailed. At the same
time investment in industry as a whole registered
its first appreciable decline since 1953. The value
of capital investment in machinery and equipment declined from TL 843 million in 1956 to TL 536 million
in 1958.[9] The private sector bore the brunt of this
decline as the state enterprises were granted priority in obtaining the commodities which were imported.
Consequently, only half of the private sector's total capacity was used in 1958.[10] The private sector's share of total industrial investment declined
to 57.2 per cent and its share of industrial capacity to 81.8 per cent. Only the production of those
industries which rely heavily upon domestically
produced raw materials maintained a steady increase.

Between 1950 and 1958, public investment accounted for about 45 per cent of total gross investment in Turkey. The greatest proportion of this investment, 72.4 per cent, went into the creation of
multipurpose projects and the development of electric power, transportation, mining, and manufacturing facilities. The largest share of private investment, 86.8 per cent, was channeled into agriculture, small industry, and construction. Table 8
indicates the distribution of investment between the
public and private sectors.

TABLE 8

Distribution of Gross Public and Private
Investment in Turkey, 1950-58

(In millions of lira)

	Public Sector	Per Cent of Total	Private Sector	Per Cent of Total	Total
Agriculture	1,466	12.6	4,153	29.0	5,619
Mining	271	2.3	22	0.2	293
Manufacturing	2,218	19.0	3,415	23.9	5,630
Construction	33	0.3	4,744	33.2	4,777
Electricity, gas and water	1,653	14.2	75	0.5	1,728
Transport and communications	4,322	37.2	1,220	8.6	5,542
Commerce	87	0.8	389	2.7	476
Services	1,582	13.6	78	0.5	1,660
Miscellaneous	3	--	204	1.4	207
Totals	11,632	100.0	14,300	100.0	25,932

Source: U.N., Economic Developments in the
Middle East 1958-1959 (New York: 1960), p. 45.

A major share of public investment is undertaken
through the regular budget. During the period 1950-
58, the government spent TL 6.5 billion in this manner for economic development purposes.[11] The budget
allocations for economic development in 1959 and
1960 totaled TL 4,829 million. These allocations
contrast sharply with average annual allocations of
TL 688 million during the period 1951-55. The budgets of the provinces, the municipalities, and the
state-owned enterprises are not included in these
allocations. A large part of the government's investment expenditures was financed with credit from
the Central Bank.

Investment in the private sector is undertaken
largely through investment of savings. Most businesses or corporations in Turkish industry are either
family-owned or operated by an individual entrepreneur and generally depend upon personal savings for
their investments. Credits obtained from commercial
banks provide another source of investment in agriculture and industry. In 1960, the Agricultural
Bank provided credits to agriculture totaling about
TL 2.4 billion. However, only about 15 per cent
represented medium-term and long-term loans.

In 1950, an Industrial Development Bank (IDB)
was created to assist in establishing new private
industrial enterprises, to help in the expansion and
modernization of existing firms, and to aid in the
development of a capital market in Turkey. The initial capital of the IDB, totaling TL 93.4 million,
consisted of TL 19 million contributed by private
domestic sources, a TL 20 million loan from the
IBRD, and TL 54.5 million obtained from Marshall
Plan counterpart funds. By December, 1960, the IDB
had approved loans totaling TL 317 million to 452
industrial enterprises.

Foreign Private Investment

In spite of periodic legislation to encourage
foreign investment, foreign private capital has not
been an important source of investment funds in
Turkey. The Law of the Encouragement of Foreign

Investments, passed in 1950, granted to foreign investors similar rights, facilities, and exemptions
as those extended to local investors. Foreign-owned
enterprises were permitted to transfer up to 10 per
cent annually of the capital invested in the form of
profits, interest, and dividends. The government
also guaranteed to make available the foreign exchange to be repatriated.[12]

In 1954, further legislation was introduced
which eliminated most of the remaining restrictions
on foreign capital and permitted, upon liquidation
of an enterprise, the transfer of all profits and
capital invested. In 1957, the government of Turkey
signed an agreement with the U.S. under which the
former guaranteed the convertibility and repatria-
tion of capital and earnings of U.S. investors,
thereby enabling them to insure their investments
with the ICA against currency inconvertibility and
loss by expropriation.

But the measures taken to attract foreign private capital had little success. Balance-of-payments
figures indicate that long-term investments totaling
only $9 million annually flowed into Turkey between
1950 and 1960. Such a low level of foreign private
investment was due, in large part, to a lack of confidence on the part of foreign investors. This was
particularly true during the first few years after
the Democratic Party was elected in 1950, when foreign investors waited for further proof of the government's willingness to accommodate private investment. After 1954, Turkey's declining rate of economic growth, its balance-of-payments difficulties, and
serious inflation served to inhibit further foreign
investment. The requirement that all investment en-
tering Turkey must be deemed propitious to the economic development of the country also was a restrain-
ing factor to many foreign investors. The continuing
presence of the public sector in most industries,
the prevailing fear of expropriation, inflation,
chronic foreign-exchange shortages, the generally
low level of per capita income, and political instability added other obstacles to an increase in the
flow of foreign capital.

PLANNING FOR ECONOMIC DEVELOPMENT,
1960-65

The Turkish military coup of May, 1960, was partly a reaction to a general dissatisfaction with the haphazard and inflationary economic policies pursued by the Menderes Regime. After 1953, the rate of economic growth slowed considerably while inflation plagued the Turkish economy. Between 1954 and 1959, the money supply expanded by 160 per cent and domestic prices more than doubled. One of the primary causes of inflation in Turkey was the large deficits of the State Economic Enterprises (SEE) which were financed largely by central and commercial bank credit.

In its external accounts, Turkey's balance-of-payments deficits became chronic and its external debt rose from about $190 million in 1952 to $930 million in 1960. Its foreign-exchange reserves were exhausted and currency devalued. Little had been done during these years to improve agricultural yields and to expand exports. Consequently, Turkey's exports tended to stagnate between $300 million and $350 million annually.

As far as the development program was concerned, there was a general feeling that a more orderly and planned development effort was required. In September, 1960, a State Planning Organization (SPO) was created with the responsibility for drawing up a development program with a fifteen-year perspective. The concept of planning was incorporated in the new 1961 Constitution. An interim plan was devised for 1962 and a five-year plan formulated to begin in 1963.[13]

The First Five-Year Plan (1963-67)

According to the "Objectives and Strategy of the Plan," the Turkish first five-year plan seeks to achieve an annual growth rate of about 7 per cent annually (40 per cent cumulatively) within the framework of a mixed economy. Of a total of TL 59.4

billion planned for investment during the course of
the plan, 22.3 per cent has been allocated to industry and mining and 17.7 per cent to agriculture.
Approximately 60 per cent of planned investment is
to be undertaken by the public sector. Table 9 details the primary objectives of the plan.

In order to achieve the plan's objectives, government planners envisage an increase in investment
from 16.3 per cent of GNP in 1962, to 19.4 per cent
in 1967, or 10.7 per cent annually.[14] During the
same period, average savings are expected to increase
from 12.3 per cent of GNP to 16.5 per cent. During
the course of the plan, imports are expected to rise
from $560 million to $704 million while exports increase from $325 million to $457 million. The role
of foreign assistance, therefore, is crucial in meeting these deficits. It is expected that the amount
of foreign financing required during the plan will
total about $1.8 billion, or $360 million annually.
By the end of the fifteen-year plan period, however,
it is expected that Turkey will be able to dispense
with foreign economic assistance.

The Plan's Progress, 1963-65

During the first three years of the plan, growth
in Turkey averaged about 5.7 per cent annually.[15]
The plan got off to a good start as GNP rose approximately 7.5 per cent in 1963, largely as a result of
a bumper crop. The leveling off of agricultural
production in 1964, however, and a consequent slow-
down in private business resulted in a relatively
smaller increase of 4.5 per cent. Cereal production
declined 20 per cent in 1964. A slight increase in
agricultural production in 1965 pushed the gain in
GNP to about 5.3 per cent. Increases in non-
agricultural production were relatively constant
but were below the planned average annual increases
of 9 per cent. Such production rose 7.5 per cent in
1963, 6.8 per cent in 1964, and 7.7 per cent in 1965.

Balance-of-payments difficulties continued to
plague the Turkish development effort, although
their severity tended to decrease somewhat during

TABLE 9

Five-Year Plan Sectoral Investment and Growth

(in billions of lira)

	Planned Investment 1963-67	Planned Production 1962	Planned Production 1967	Annual Increase Planned 1963-67 (Per Cent)	Annual Increase Actual 1950-62 (Per Cent)
Productive sectors					
Agriculture	10.5	34.7	43.6	4.7	3.4
Mining and quarrying	3.2	2.3	3.6	8.7	3.9
Manufacturing	10.1	18.2	31.5	11.5	5.7
Energy	5.1	0.6	1.2	12.8	15.1
Transportation and communication	8.0	3.4	5.3	9.6	9.1
Nonproductive sectors					
Services	4.0				
Housing	12.2				
Education	4.2				
Health	1.3				
Tourism	0.8				
Total Investment	59.6				

Source: Republic of Turkey, First Five-Year Development Plan of Turkey 1963-1967 (Ankara: State Planning Organization, 1963).

the first three years of the plan. During these
years exports rose sharply, reaching $411 million
in 1964 and $459 million in 1965. Imports, on the
other hand, totaled $538 million in 1964 and $572
million in 1965. The increase in exports in 1965,
however, was largely a result of a jump in bilateral trade with Soviet Bloc countries.

Turkey continued to rely heavily on external
financing during the first three years of the plan.
The amount of foreign aid required to cover the
balance-of-payments deficit totaled about $400 mil-
lion annually.[16] An additional $530 million was
required during the three-year period to cover principal and interest payments on Turkey's foreign
debt. The inflow of foreign private capital averaged only about $25 million annually.

THE ROLE OF U.S. ECONOMIC ASSISTANCE

Economic assistance provided by the U.S. has
been an important source of finance for Turkish
economic development since 1950. In April, 1948,
the Economic Cooperation Administration (ECA) was
established to assist the war-ravaged countries of
Europe with their reconstruction programs. The
newly created Organization for European Economic
Cooperation (OEEC) was given the responsibility for
coordinating the aid programs, subsequently known
as the Marshall Plan for Europe. The participating
countries directed their efforts toward four main
targets: (1) an increase in total production;
(2) stabilization of the international monetary system; (3) cooperation of the participating countries
in the development of Europe's economic resources;
and (4) expansion of exports as a solution to their
balance-of-payments difficulties.[17]

That these goals were paramount in the thinking
of ECA officials when aid to Turkey was initiated
was specifically pointed out in a study of Turkish
economic aid requirements. Discussing the problems
of selecting projects to receive economic assistance,
the report stated:

> [In] the selection of industrial proj-
> ects, the general policy of ECA is to
> restrict its financing to those projects
> that are not only economically and do-
> mestically advantageous, but which are
> also directly or indirectly helpful to
> the other participating countries. . . . .
> The final criterion must be in each in-
> stance that Turkey will contribute to
> European recovery.[18]

Turkey's requirements for economic assistance,
however, differed from those of the other members of
the OEEC in that they were related to the need for
economic development rather than reconstruction.
Consequently, it was necessary not only to expand
the production of agriculture and the extractive industries, but first to create the necessary infrastructure. It was expected that investments in agriculture, mining, electric power, and transportation
not only would lead to higher future levels of production but also would provide agricultural surpluses
which could be exchanged for the industrial products
of Western Europe.[19]

Types of U.S. Economic Assistance

The U.S. has been providing large-scale economic assistance to Turkey since the enactment of the
Greek-Turkish Assistance Act of May 22, 1947. Beginning in April, 1948, economic assistance to
Turkey was included under the allocations for the
European Recovery Program. In October, 1951, assistance to Turkey became a part of the Mutual Security Program. By the end of June, 1965, the U.S.
had extended $2,279 million in loans, credits, and
grants to assist Turkey in carrying out economic development projects and in supporting the Turkish
contribution to NATO. Table 10 details the types
of economic assistance Turkey has received from the
U.S.

TABLE 10

U.S. Economic Aid to Turkey,
FY 1946-FY 1965

(In millions of dollars)

U.S. Fiscal Years	Total Aid	AID and Predecessor Agencies	P.L. 480 Agricultural Commodities	Export-Import Bank	Other
1946-48	44.5	...	...	32.3	12.2
1949-52	225.1	225.1	...	...	...
1953-57	512.8	394.0	113.2	5.6	...
1958	130.8	81.7	49.1	...	...
1959	216.4	141.8	37.2	37.4	...
1960	126.1	91.5	34.6	...	...
1961	225.8	200.1	25.7	...	...
1962	208.7	70.8	137.8	...	0.1
1963	187.8	127.5	59.6	...	0.7
1964	189.9	125.9	62.4	...	1.6
1965	211.9	149.8	59.1	...	3.0
Totals	2,279.8	1,608.2	578.7	75.3	17.6

Source: U.S. Overseas Loans and Grants.

In addition to the assistance provided to pay
for imported goods and services, local currencies
generated by certain portions of U.S. economic assistance have been an important source of funds for
financing the domestic costs of economic development
and defense. These funds are accumulated as a result of counterpart arrangements and P.L. 480 commodity sales. As of June 30, 1964, TL 4.8 billion
in counterpart funds had been allocated for specific
use in Turkey.[20] Allocations for military purposes
accounted for 61 per cent of these funds. The balance was allocated for a variety of economic purposes. In addition, P.L. 480 local currencies
totaling more than TL 1.9 billion were programmed
for use in Turkey.

Sectoral Distribution of U.S. Aid

A precise sectoral distribution of U.S. economic
assistance is not possible as a large part of such
aid has been provided for balance-of-payments purposes. Commodities received by Turkey under the aid
program enter the country in the same manner as regular imports and, consequently, it is not possible
to determine the destination of many of these commodities. A reasonable order of magnitude may be
devised, however, by allocating specific commodity
categories to the sectors in which they are likely
to be used.

Agriculture

By the end of fiscal year 1965, U.S. aid committed for the agricultural sector totaled about
$135 million. Turkey received agricultural machine-
ry, equipment, and spare parts totaling $87.9 mil-
lion. During the years of large investment in
agriculture, i.e., 1950-55, U.S. aid was the source
of 20 per cent of the tractors imported for use in
Turkey.[21] Other commodities which can be directly
allocated for use in the agricultural sector totaled about $10 million. An additional $9 million
was obligated for various technical assistance programs.

In 1952, the government launched a $40 million
program to construct storage facilities for the increase in grain production which was expected to
result from the development of the agricultural sector.   The construction of these facilities was one
of the more important agricultural projects financed
with U.S. aid. By the end of June, 1957, $16.1 mil-
lion had been obligated for the purchase and construction of these facilities.[22] A loan of $4.2
million also was obtained from the Export-Import
Bank in 1954 to purchase grain storage and handling
equipment. During this period, silo capacity increased from 429,000 tons to 1.1 million tons and
reached approximately 1.8 million tons in 1960.

Unfortunately, the grain storage program was
predicated upon the expectation of a continuing high
level of production and large surpluses available
for export. In April, 1957, only 45,000 tons of
wheat were in storage, practically all imported.
Freighters unloading this wheat in Istanbul were
required to transfer their cargo to lighters because
the modern, completely automatic grain silo was designed for exports and not for imports.[23]

Transportation and Communication

Aid obligations for the development of transportation and communication facilities totaled about
$215 million by the end of June, 1965. Such aid has
been particularly significant in the development of
a highway system in Turkey. Between 1948 and the
end of 1959, Turkey invested about TL 2.8 billion in
highway construction.[24] The U.S. contribution during
this period totaled about $50 million and represented
as much as 15 per cent of the total cost of the Turkish road program. By the end of 1959, Turkey had
completed 60,623 miles of new highway with U.S. assistance.[25]

Industry and Mining

U.S. aid expenditures have been a major source
of funds for investment in industrial and mineral development in Turkey. Obligations for these sectors

during the fiscal years 1950-65 totaled at least
$880 million. Aid commitments for machinery, equip-
ment, industrial raw materials, and semimanufactured
products under nonproject import programs amounted
to more than $660 million. Much of the development
of Turkey's mineral industry since 1950 has been accomplished with U.S. economic assistance. By the
end of June, 1965, this sector had been allocated
about $125 million.

Technical Assistance

A highly significant component of the U.S. aid
program in Turkey has been the provision of technical assistance. Although the cost of this program
has been relatively small, its effective implementation has been essential for the efficacy of the
Turkish development program. Between 1948 and mid-
1965, $53.9 million was programmed for technical
assistance. The program has made available the
services of American experts in many fields and has
trained Turkish nationals employed in those fields
at institutions in the U.S. Education, transportation, and agriculture have received the largest
share of the allocations, about $28 million.

During fiscal years 1955-64, 1,785 Turkish nationals were sent to the U.S. for various periods of
intensive training under the technical assistance
program. In addition, AID and its predecessor agencies contracted with several U.S. universities to
provide similar training for 217 individuals.

Technical assistance for the development of the
transportation system may serve as an example of the
importance of this form of aid. A total of $6.4
million was obligated for this sector. Between July,
1954, and June, 1964, a total of 158 Turkish nationals were trained at installations in the U.S. under
the participant training program. A major part of
the technical services provided by the Bureau of
Public Roads in connection with the road construction program was a training program for Turkish nationals. On-the-job training was provided for more
than 5,000 technical personnel for the construction

phases of road building and maintenance projects.
In the process, 55 fully equipped repair shops were
established throughout Turkey and 70 employees of
the Highway Directorate were educated in the U.S.
in economics, engineering, and accounting.[26]

ASSESSMENT AND IMPACT

U.S. Economic Aid as a Source
of Investment Funds

Expenditures under the U.S. aid program have
been an important addition to the total resources
available for capital formation in Turkey. These
funds have played a particularly significant part
in the development of transportation, industrial,
and electric power facilities. During the years
1950-64, for example, aid expenditures totaled an
equivalent of TL 12.8 billion, equal to 17 per cent
of gross investment in Turkey.[27] Table 11 outlines
the distribution of U.S. aid and total investment in
Turkey.

It is unlikely that Turkey would have experienced any significant increase in real income (at
least since the mid-1950's) had it not been for the
availability of U.S. economic aid. Although real
per capita income, for example, increased 36.3 per
cent during the 1950's, most of the increase occurred during the first four years of the decade,
when U.S. aid still was not a crucial source of
funds. The bulk of U.S. aid expenditures occurred
after 1953. If U.S. economic assistance had not
been available as a supplemental source of investment, the level of domestic investment obviously
would have declined sharply. This impact is in addition to the indirect effect of the savings in
foreign exchange which resulted from the import of
U.S. agricultural commodities and the diversion of
much of this foreign exchange to the purchase of
goods and services required for the development
program.

TABLE 11

Relation of U.S. Aid to Gross Investment in Turkey, 1950-64

(In millions of lira)

	Total Gross Investment 1950-60	Total Gross Public Investment 1950-60	U.S. Economic Aid Expenditures	U.S. Economic Aid Per Cent of Total Investment	Per Cent of Public Investment
Agriculture	13,845	5,208	760	5	14
Industry and mining	17,704	7,197)			
Electric power and other utilities	4,834	4,615)	7,052	31	59
Transportation and communication	14,127	11,552	1,241	9	11
Other	23,279	8,284	3,789	16	46
Totals	73,789	36,856	12,843	17	35

Source: Republic of Turkey, Budget Speech by Minister of Finance (Ankara: Ministry of Finance, 1953-60); AID, Operations Report as of June 30, 1965; Export-Import Bank of Washington, Statement of Authorized Loans and Credits, July 31, 1965; AID, Status of Loans as of December 31, 1965; various issues of the Turkish Economic Review, 1964-65.

U.S. Economic Aid and the Public Sector

In spite of official Turkish statements of support for an expanding role for private investment, state participation continues to dominate Turkish economic development. The pervading influence of government-owned enterprises has found considerable support in the economic assistance received from the U.S. The importance of such aid to the public sector is indicated in Table 11 above. Total U.S. aid is equivalent to 35 per cent of total public investment and is particularly significant in the industrial and mining sectors.

Although the difficulty of determining the amount of assistance allocated directly to the respective sectors prevents a precise analysis of the flow of aid funds, it is unlikely that more than 15 per cent of U.S. aid to Turkey has been received by the country's private sector. For example, of the total of $126.5 million representing OEEC drawing rights and initial position credits and contributions to Turkey's European Payments Union quota assessed prior to 1951, only $2 million were made available to the private sector.[28] Particularly striking in the same connection is that of the total of $75.3 million in Export-Import Bank loans to Turkey, none were to private interests.

It has been pointed out that by the end of June, 1958, MSP economic assistance provided to private interests in the agricultural sector accounted for 20.9 per cent of total U.S. aid to that sector.[29] Only 7 per cent of the TL 74.5 million in counterpart currency allocated up to that time for the industrial sector was provided to the private sector.[30] Most of the funds loaned directly to private firms by the ECA were disbursed prior to 1950.[31] The major portion of the total of counterpart funds provided for government activities in the industrial sector, TL 54.5 million, was used as part of the capital required to establish the Industrial Development Bank in 1950. The funds used for the IDB, however, were subsequently reloaned to the

private sector. Of the total of TL 1.9 billion set
aside for country use from the sale of P.L. 480 commodities, only 16.9 per cent was earmarked for private interests.

Steps have been taken, however, to channel more
of U.S. aid to the private sector. The DLF loan of
$129 million for the Eregli iron and steel works in
1961, for example, was extended to private interests
to be used in conjunction with funds provided by
private foreign investors. A joint Turkish-American
company was established to operate the steel works.
The Turkish Government subscribed to 48 per cent of
the capital shares of the company. Four U.S. firms
were to purchase 30 per cent of the remaining shares
and private Turkish interests, 22 per cent.[32] In
February, 1961, an agreement was concluded with ICA
for the creation of a Mining Assistance Commission.
This commission was established to assist in expanding the private sector's activities in the mineral
industry and to encourage foreign private investment
in the development of Turkey's mineral resources.
The U.S. agreed to finance the exploration, development, and operation of mineral projects considered
to be sound business ventures.[33] Early in 1961, ICA
established a revolving fund with a capital of TL 5.5
million in counterpart currency to encourage small
private businesses by making available to these enterprises sources of long-term credit.[34]

U.S. Aid and Turkish Inflation

Economic assistance has been an important contributing factor in the inflation which prevailed in
Turkey during the 1950's. The inflow of large sums
of dollar aid and the release of substantial amounts
of counterpart funds certainly stimulated economic
activity. But these funds also encouraged a more
rapid increase in the supply of money and the volume
of credit. The counterpart funds were a particularly important source of funds for the State Economic
Enterprises and were used to finance a large part of
the operating deficits of these organizations. They
had authority to engage in unlimited borrowing of

these funds from domestic banks and, consequently,
were important contributors to the inflationary
spiral.

Perhaps the most serious problem was the gradual shift from aid primarily for development purposes to financing the deficit on current account.
Prior to 1955, Turkey's balance-of-payments deficit
was financed mainly by short-term commercial credits
and drawings on foreign-exchange reserves. Subsequent deficits during the 1950's, however, were covered by U.S. aid, foreign credits, and infrastructure
and offshore procurement transactions. As the character of U.S. aid shifted from capital goods for investment to the provision of raw materials, spare
parts, and surplus commodities, aid was utilized much
more to support the current operations of the Turkish
economy. After 1961, the aid portion included some
outlays of European consortium countries. The relative shares of the two categories used to finance the
balance-of-payments deficit are presented in Table 12.

Continuing Need for Economic Aid

It appears unlikely that Turkey will be able to
achieve a rate of economic growth over the fifteen-
year plan period to enable it to dispense with foreign economic aid. The goal of increasing GNP at a
rate of 7 per cent annually is optimistic. During
the last half of the 1950's, GNP grew at an average
annual rate of about 4 per cent. Although the
growth rate during the first three years of the current plan was not unfavorable, it fell short of the
plan's objective.

Plans to increase investment to 19.4 per cent of
GNP by 1967 also appear unrealistic. The rate of investment during the 1950's averaged about 14 per cent
of GNP. During the years 1961-64, the rate of investment appears to have increased only slightly.
Moreover, the level of gross investment called for
in the plan is predicated on the expectation that
domestic private investment will increase substantially. The trend of this investment prior to the

plan, however, was downward. The private sector accounted for 49 per cent of total investment in 1959,
45 per cent in 1960, and 41 per cent in 1961.[35]
Without the higher level of investment, and the
larger incomes and potential savings it generates,
foreign aid will have to continue to fill the gap.
Meanwhile, with population increasing at about 3 per
cent annually, a larger share of each year's investment will have to be channeled into nonproductive
undertakings.

TABLE 12

Sources of Finance for Turkey's
Balance-of-Payments Deficits

(Per cent of total)

Fiscal Year	Foreign Exchange, Grants, and Long-Term Loans, Offshore and Infrastructure Operations	Short- and Medium-Term Loans
1952-53	72*	28
1953-54	18	82
1954-55	40	60
1955-56	61	39
1956-57	69	31
1957-58	62	38
1958-59	76	24
1959-60	82	18
1960-61	76	24
1961-62	79	21
1962-63	81	19

*Primarily outlays of foreign exchange.

Source: Industrial Development Bank of Turkey,
Annual Statement, December 31, 1955, through December 31, 1963.

Notes to Chapter 3

1. International Bank for Reconstruction and Development, The Economy of Turkey (Baltimore: Johns Hopkins Press, 1951), p. 6.

2. Kurt Grunwald and Joachim O. Ronall, Industrialization in the Middle East (New York: Council for Middle Eastern Affairs Press, 1960), p. 336.

3. Memduh Yasa, "The Denationalization of the Government Enterprises," Paper Presented at the Kilyos Conference, Turkey, July, 1959, p. 3. (Mimeographed.)

4. U.S. Economic Cooperation Administration, Turkey Country Study (Washington: 1949), p. 29.

5. U.S. Department of Agriculture, Report No. 106, Agricultural Development in Turkey (Washington: 1958), p. 1.

6. Harvey Oakes, The Soils of Turkey (Ankara: 1957). Quoted in United Nations, FAO Mediterranean Development Project (Rome: Food and Agriculture Organization, 1959), p. 207.

7. Organization for European Economic Cooperation, Turkey 1958, EC(59)10 (Paris: 1959), p. 12.

8. "The Democratic Party Election Manifesto," Middle Eastern Affairs, I (May, 1950), 150.

9. United Nations, Economic Developments in the Middle East 1957-1958 (New York: 1959), p. 25.

10. Turkey 1958, p. 12.

11. Republic of Turkey, Budget Speech by Minister of Finance, February 20, 1959, Publication No. 1959-60:99-1 (Ankara: Ministry of Finance, 1959), p. 72.

12.   Cihat Iren, "Foreign Capital Investment in Turkey," Turkish Economic Review, I (February, 1960), 4.

13.   The British Chamber of Commerce of Turkey, Monthly Trade Journal (Istanbul), June-July, 1961, p. 89.

14.   Organization of Economic Cooperation and Development, Turkey (Paris: 1963), p. 13.

15.   Turkey (Paris: 1966), p. 49.

16.   Ibid., p. 46.

17.   Harry Bayard Price, The Marshall Plan and its Meaning (Ithaca: Cornell University Press, 1955), p. 37.

18.   Turkey Country Study, p. 30.

19.   Ibid., p. 4.

20.   The actual total of lira counterpart funds should be much larger.   The dollar equivalents of counterpart liras deposited have, on occasion, been based on an exchange rate lower than the official rate.   The utilization of counterpart funds presented in Turkish Economic Statistics of 1961, for example, indicated an exchange rate of $1 = TL 4.9, as opposed to the official rate of TL 9.

21.   W. H. Nicholls, "Investment in Agriculture in Underdeveloped Countries," American Economic Review, XLV (May, 1955), 67.

22.   Comptroller General of the United States, Examination of Economic and Technical Assistance Program for Turkey, June 30, 1957, Report to the Congress of the United States (Washington: 1958), p.51.

23.   Agricultural Development in Turkey, p. 17.

24. Malcolm D. Rivkin, Area Development for National Growth (New York: Frederick A. Praeger, 1965), p. 108.

25. Ibid., p. 109.

26. Examination of Economic and Technical Assistance Program for Turkey, p. 59.

27. The lira figure represents U.S. aid expenditures converted at the official rates of exchange which prevailed during the relevant years. Consequently, the contribution of the U.S. may be understated.

28. Republic of Turkey, Quarterly Report on the Marshall Plan in Turkey, No. 7 (Ankara: Office for International Cooperation, 1951), p. 13.

29. Bulent Yazici, "Problems of United States Economic Aid to Turkey," Paper delivered at the Kilyos Conference, Turkey, July, 1959. (Mimeographed.)

30. Ibid.

31. Quarterly Report on the Marshall Plan in Turkey, No. 9 (1951), p. 45; No. 33 (1957), p. 42.

32. Middle East Economic Digest, January 29, 1960, p. 45.

33. Turkish Economic Review, I (March, 1961),8.

34. Ibid., p. 23.

35. IKA Agency, Economic and Commercial News Agency, "Five-Year Development Plan of Turkey 1963-1967," Monthly Report No. 1 (Ankara: September, 1962), p. 16. (Mimeographed.)

CHAPTER

4

INDIA: FOCUS OF
MAJOR U.S. AND
U.S.S.R. PROGRAMS

Since attaining its independence in 1947, India
has been faced with the monumental task of raising
per capita income in the face of a rapidly increasing population. Large sums have been expended on a
development program, the aim of which has been to
double real national income in less than twenty
years (between 1950 and 1968) and per capita income
by 1974. In April, 1951, the Indian Government
launched the first of a series of five-year plans
designed to achieve these goals.

ECONOMIC PLANNING AND THE PUBLIC SECTOR

The Recent History of Economic
Planning in India

The genesis of modern economic planning in
India may be said to date from 1931, when the Indian National Congress discussed the matter at length
in its Karachi Session. The Congress leaders, in-
spired by the Soviet experience, recommended a program of state economic planning to eliminate poverty
in India.[1] The first positive step, however, was
not taken until October, 1938, when a conference of
Ministers of Industries adopted a resolution stating
that industrialization was the key to economic
growth in India. A National Planning Commission
(NPC) was created, with Jawaharlal Nehru as its
chairman, and charged with the responsibility for
developing such a plan. But the NPC could present
nothing of value, claiming a plan could not be formulated until independence was obtained.

69

In January, 1944, a group of Indian industrialists, seeking to counter the growing influence of those calling for greater state participation in India's economic development, presented a Plan of Economic Development of India, known as the "Bombay Plan." This plan envisaged a fifteen-year investment program designed to produce a threefold increase in national income. Primary emphasis was placed on industrialization, as 45 per cent of suggested investment was allocated to that sector. But while a planned approach to economic development was recommended, the private sector was expected to play the major role in that program. The activities of the state were to be confined to coordination and tax collection.[2]

Several months later, in April, 1944, the Indian Federation of Labour published a People's Plan for Economic Development in India which held the existing system of production to be the real cause of poverty in India and recommended the replacement of the capitalist economic system with a socialist type. The People's Plan called for a much higher level of investment over a period of ten years than was recommended in the Bombay Plan. Agriculture, however, was allocated a greater share of total investment.

In 1946, the government of India's postwar Reconstruction Committee presented a vague fifteen-year plan with objectives not significantly different from the earlier nonofficial plans. The only concrete result stemming from this committee's report was the establishment of an Advisory Planning Board with the responsibility for reviewing the functions of the existing planning bodies in India and monitoring whatever planning machinery might be established in the future. The board accomplished little, but the government's present industrial policies are based largely on the board's recommendations.

Immediately after attaining independence, a variety of development projects were launched by the

central and state governments. In order to avoid
duplication in these undertakings, the Indian Planning Commission (IPC) was created in 1949. As set
forth in the Indian Constitution, the IPC was as-
signed the general responsibility for advancing the
welfare of the Indian people by "securing" social,
economic, and political justice and was empowered to
assess India's resources, formulate a plan of priorities for their use, appraise the progress of developmental activities, and make any recommendations
and adjustments it considered necessary.[3]

Before the IPC could initiate action toward the
formulation of a comprehensive plan, it was called
upon to present a six-year plan to be incorporated
into the Colombo Plan for Cooperative Development of
South and Southeast Asia. The requirements presented by India were modest and of relatively little
importance. The plan's major features, however, subsequently served as a basis for the formulation of
the first five-year plan.[4]

The Goals of Planning

A major objective of India's economic development program is the creation of a "socialist pattern
of society." According to Indian officials, this
means:

> . . . that the basic criterion for de-
> termining the lines of advance must
> not be private profits but social gain,
> and that . . . the structure of socio-
> economic relations should be so planned
> that they result . . . in greater equal-
> ity in income and wealth.[5]

The achievement of such a society also implies
long-run changes in the basic economic and social
structure of India, since the government's task is
not only to redistribute income within the existing
economic and social framework but also to change
that framework in the process. The IPC states:

> The task before an underdeveloped coun-
> try is not merely to get better results
> within the existing framework of eco-
> nomic and social institutions but to
> mold and refashion these so that they
> contribute effectively to the realiza-
> tion of wider and deeper social values.[6]

Indian officials seek to bring about this socialist transformation within the framework of planned
economic development and by expanding the economic
activities of the public sector. One Indian author
states:

> A progressive widening of the public
> sector is an essential pre-requisite
> of any progress towards a socialist
> society, particularly in an underde-
> veloped area undertaking rapid planned
> development. . . . It is extremely
> important to remember that the improve-
> ments that are desired, in distribution
> of incomes and in the standards of liv-
> ing of the poorest classes in India,
> can best be brought about by an appro-
> priate distribution of constructive
> activities and orientation of the pro-
> duction organization . . .[7]

Indian plans provide for a rapid growth of the
public sector, not only absolutely, but also relatively to the private sector. Although private
enterprise is expected to play an important part in
India's economic development, it must be done within the framework of the comprehensive plan. Indian
officials not only believe that the government must
play the dominant role in shaping the entire pattern
of Indian investment but must also initiate investments which the private sector is either unwilling or
unable to undertake.

In the Indian drive to achieve the goals of the
development program, industrialization has received
a high priority. Industrial development in India is

governed by the Industrial Policy Resolution of
April, 1956. The resolution cites the broad goals
of reducing disparities of wealth and of preventing
monopolies and stresses the necessity to accelerate
the rate of economic growth, speed industrialization
by developing heavy industries, and expand the public sector. The resolution further states:

> The adoption of the socialist pattern
> of society . . . requires that all in-
> dustries of basic and strategic im-
> portance, or in the nature of public
> utility services, should be in the
> public sector.[8]

The industrial sector is divided into three categories, each based on the projected role of the government in the respective category. The first category includes seventeen industries in which the public sector has exclusive responsibility for future
development, although existing private enterprises
in these industries are permitted to expand. These
industries include defense, atomic energy, metallur-
gy, machine building, coal, mining and processing of
most ores, major transportation equipment, communications equipment, and electric power distribution.

The second category consists of twelve industries which will gradually come under the public
sector's domination as the state establishes new
enterprises in these industries. Private enterprise, however, is expected to supplement the effort
of the public sector in these industries. This category includes the production of most other minerals,
aluminum, machine tools, basic chemical products,
pharmaceuticals, fertilizers, certain ferroalloys,
and some transportation equipment.

The third category includes all other industries but does not specify them. Although development of industries in this category is left to the
private sector, the government still retains the
prerogative of also establishing new industries.

THE FIVE-YEAR PLANS

Growth of National Income

between the initiation of the development plans in India in 1951 and early 1964, real national income increased 68.7 per cent, an average annual rate of increase of 3.8 per cent. This increase, however, has not been constant and is less than the originally planned annual increase of 5 per cent. Table 13 presents the growth of Indian national income during the five-year plans.

When the first five-year plan was launched, national income was expected to rise from about Rs. 9,000 crores to Rs. 10,000 crores, or 11.1 per cent by mid-1961.[9] The actual increase in national income, however, substantially exceeded the planned increase, rising 18.4 per cent. But this growth was not constant; a rise of almost 13 per cent was registered during the first three years of the plan, largely as a result of a substantial increase in agricultural production. During the last two years of the first plan, the rate of increase dropped sharply.

The relative success of the first plan prompted the government to set more ambitious goals for the second five-year plan (April, 1956-March, 1961). The target established was an increase in real national income of 25 per cent.[10] The actual increase in national income during the second plan amounted to 21.1 per cent. The third five-year plan (April, 1961-March, 1966) envisaged an increase in national income of more than 5 per cent annually, which, according to the Indian Government, would result in a total increase of 80 per cent in national income during the period of the three plans.

Population Growth and Per Capita Income

The growth of population is perhaps the greatest obstacle facing India in its efforts to create the conditions for self-sustaining growth. Any effort

TABLE 13

Growth of National Income in India,*

FY 1951-FY 1965

(In crores of rupees**)

Indian Fiscal Years (April-March)	Agriculture	Industry & Mining	Commerce, Transportation, and Communication	Other	Net Earned Income from Abroad	Totals	Per Cent Change
1950-51	4,340	1,480	1,660	1,390	-20	8,850	
1955-56	5,020	1,760	1,970	1,730	0	10,480	
1956-57	5,250	1,840	2,080	1,820	10	11,000	+3.5
1957-58	5,010	1,860	2,110	1,920	-10	10,890	-1.0
1958-59	5,560	1,880	2,190	2,040	-20	11,650	+6.9
1959-60	5,500	1,970	2,270	2,140	-30	11,850	+1.7
1960-61	5,900	2,110	2,460	2,310	-50	12,730	+7.4
1961-62	5,910	2,210	2,540	2,470	-80	13,060	+2.6
1962-63	5,800	2,310	2,640	2,700	-80	13,370	+2.4
1963-64	5,900	2,440	2,770	2,890	-90	13,910	+4.0
1964-65	6,440	2,540	2,930	3,120	-10	14,930	+7.3

*At 1948-49 prices.   **One crore equals $2.1 million.

Source: Government of India, Review of the First Five Year Plan (New Delhi: Planning Commission, 1957), p. 7; Report on Currency and Finance for the Year 1961-62 (Bombay: Reserve Bank of India, 1962), Statement 10; Economic Survey 1965-66 (New Delhi: Ministry of Finance, 1966), Table 1.1.

to raise individual income and the standard of living, to relieve unemployment and the pressure on the land, and to provide essential social services continually is frustrated by the rapid increase in India's population. This is reflected in the relatively small growth in per capita income. In the years between the initiation of the first plan in 1951 and 1965, per capita income rose 20.9 per cent. While the average annual rate of increase of national income was 3.8 per cent, the rate of increase in per capita income averaged only 1.9 per cent. The growth in per capita income is presented in Table 14.

The original expectation concerning the planned growth in per capita income was predicated on an estimated annual increase in India's population of 1.25 per cent. In 1957, Indian officials predicted that by the end of the second plan the Indian population would increase by 25 million people.[11] During the ten years of the first two plans, however, the actual growth totaled 77.5 million, representing an average annual increase of about 2.5 per cent. Official estimates subsequently were revised to reflect an annual increase of 8 million people during the third plan, compared with an earlier estimate of 5 million. U.N. figures, however, indicate that the annual increase since 1958 has been about 10 million.

Public Expenditures

The national income goals originally set for India's development program called for continually increasing levels of public expenditures. During the years 1951-61, planned public outlays increased 250 per cent. Table 15 presents a sectoral distribution of public outlays during the five-year plans. The first plan generally was modest in scope. It was not as much a "plan" as a collection of projects chosen for their immediate practicality and not as elements based on priorities of an integrated nature. Although the first plan called for public outlays totaling Rs. 2,378 crores, actual expenditures were only Rs. 1,960 crores. Emphasis was placed on the development of agriculture, along with irrigation

TABLE 14

Growth of Per Capita Income in India,
1951-64

	Estimates of Midyear Population (in millions)	Per Capita Income (in rupees at 1948-49 prices)	Annual Per Cent Change
1951	362.8	248	
1952	370.6	250	+1.6
1953	378.3	256	+2.4
1954	382.9	266	+3.9
1955	390.1	268	+0.8
1956	394.2	268	0.0
1957	402.2	276	+2.9
1958	410.7	267	-3.3
1959	419.6	280	+4.9
1960	429.0	279	-0.4
1961	439.0	293	+5.0
1962	449.6	294	+0.3
1963	460.5	295*	+0.3
1964	471.6	300*	+1.7

*Estimated.

Source: United Nations, Monthly Bulletin of Statistics, January, 1961, and April, 1966, Table 1, p. 2; Economic Survey 1964-65, Table 1.1.

TABLE 15

Public Outlays on India's Five-Year Plans*
(In crores of rupees)

	1st Five-Year Plan		2nd Five-Year Plan		3rd Five-Year Plan		% Increase	
	Expenditures	% of Total	Expenditures	% of Total	Expenditures (Planned)	% of Total	2nd plan over 1st	3rd plan over 2nd
Agriculture & community development	291	15	530	11	1,068	14	82	102
Major & medium irrigation	310	16	420	9	650	9	34	55
Electric power	260	13	445	10	1,012	14	71	127
Village & small industries	43	2	175	4	264	4	81	51
Industry & mining	74	4	900	19	1,520	20	1,116	69
Transportation, communication	523	27	1,300	28	1,486	19	148	1
Social service, miscellaneous	459	23	830	19	1,300	17	81	57
Inventories	..	..	..	..	200	3	..	..
Totals	1,960	100	4,600	100	7,500	100	145	63

*Outlays include investment and current expenditures, largely for social services.

Source: Government of India, Third Five Year Plan (New Delhi: Planning Commission, 1961), pp. 33, 58.

and electric power, and transportation and communication facilities.   These sectors accounted for 71 per cent of total outlays.

The major objective of the second plan was to accelerate the rate of economic growth begun during the first plan. Toward this end, the second plan called for an increase of 204 per cent in public outlays. Actual expenditures, however, fell somewhat short of planned outlays. During the second plan greater emphasis was placed on rapid industrialization, particularly development of basic and heavy industries. Total outlay for industry and mining rose from 4 per cent to 19 per cent of total expenditures. Public outlays on transportation and communications facilities during the second plan also comprised a larger share of total expenditures than during the previous plan. The result was a sharp drop in the share allocated for the development of agriculture and related irrigation facilities.

As the level of expenditures during the second plan began to increase, the government was confronted with a shortage of funds to finance the program. Three years of bad weather, a sharp increase in imports, and a rise in the level of world prices of imported products largely contributed to India's deteriorating financial position. Furthermore, planning officials had badly miscalculated the cost of some projects and underestimated the requirements of many of the newly developed industries.[12]

These financial difficulties compelled the Indian Government to revise its original investment plans, dividing the second plan into two parts. The first part comprised an outlay of Rs. 4,500 crores on so-called core projects.   These were projects concerned with increasing agricultural production and in which substantial sums already had been invested. Priority was given to steel plants, coal production, transportation, and certain electric power projects. The second part consisted of projects totaling Rs. 300 crores, for which expenditures would be undertaken only to the extent that additional resources became available.[13] Despite the pressure on foreign-exchange reserves and the downward revision of planned outlays in all other sectors, allocations for the industrial sector increased. Total outlays in the public sector actually totaled Rs. 4,600 crores during the second plan.

In April, 1961, India embarked on the third plan with the principal goal of achieving "a major step on the road toward self-sustaining growth."[14] Planned public outlays for the third plan totaled Rs. 7,500 crores, an increase of 63 per cent over actual outlays during the second plan. The objectives of the third plan were: (1) a rise in national income of more than 5 per cent annually; (2) an increase in agricultural production to achieve self-sufficiency in food grains and meet export and domestic requirements; (3) an expansion of basic industries and establishment of machine-building capacity; (4) a substantial expansion of employment opportunities; and (5) a more equitable distribution of income.[15]

Indian officials considered their unfavorable external financial position a major obstacle to the accomplishment of their objectives. Heavy capital import requirements, added to other import needs, have placed a heavy burden on India's foreign-exchange earnings, a condition which has affected investment targets. Consequently, the Indian Government gave high priority to investments which would create capital-import substitutes and otherwise help ease balance-of-payments difficulties within a period of ten years. Although planned expenditures on the development of industrial and transportation facilities were proportionately less than the shares allocated to these sectors during the second plan, they continued to be maintained at a high level. The portion of planned total outlays on agriculture, community development, and large-scale irrigation projects was increased from 20 per cent to 23 per cent.

Development of Agriculture

Agriculture forms the mainstay of India's economic life, supporting about 70 per cent of the population and contributing about 45 per cent of India's
national income. As such, the bulk of domestic resources for India's economic development must come
from the agricultural sector. But Indian efforts to
rapidly increase agricultural production are hampered by inadequate water supplies, lack of widespread use of fertilizers, and generally inefficient
farming practices. Only about one-fifth of total
arable land in India is irrigated. As a result,
fluctuations in the amount of annual rainfall play
a crucial role in the volume of agricultural production. When rainfall is excessive, wide agricultural
areas are flooded and crops destroyed. Inadequate
rainfall and poor distribution of water, on the
other hand, restrict the amount of land which can
be double cropped.

Agricultural production in India has increased
steadily since 1950, but, because of the variability
of rainfall, has been subject to periodic fluctuations. Variations in the production of food grains
in particular have been substantial and especially
critical. The production of commercial crops also
has been expanding, but has not fluctuated to the
same extent. The growth of agricultural production
during the three plans is presented in Table 16.

When the first plan was launched, the government
budgeted 44 per cent of total outlays for the agricultural sector. The primary goal was to increase
the production of food grains from 54 million tons
to 61.6 million tons. Agricultural production increased 16.8 per cent during this period. The output of food grains and oilseeds exceeded planned
goals, but production of the important export crops--
cotton, jute, and sugar cane--fell below planned
levels. Because of exceptionally favorable weather,
food grain production reached a peak level of 68.7
million tons in 1953-54, but declined during the
last two years of the first plan.

TABLE 16

Index of Agricultural Production in India,
1950-51 Through 1964-65

(Base--June, 1950=100)

	1950-51	1955-56	1960-61	1961-62	1962-63*	1963-64*	1964-65*
General index	95.6	116.8	142.2	144.8	137.5	142.6	157.6
Food grains	90.5	115.3	137.1	140.3	130.4	135.9	149.1
Nonfood grains	105.9	119.9	152.6	153.9	151.8	156.2	174.9
Oil seeds	98.5	108.6	134.0	140.0	137.7	132.8	163.4
Fibers	108.6	149.7	176.0	187.5	193.6	207.0	201.1
Plantation crops	104.0	113.2	129.2	140.0	141.0	145.2	156.9
Miscellaneous	110.3	120.1	163.4	156.3	151.0	159.0	178.9

*Provisional.

Source: Economic Survey 1965-66, Table 1.2.

The high priority given the agricultural sector
in the allocation of resources during the first plan
was not maintained during the second plan. Although
the absolute amount of planned public outlays for
agriculture and multipurpose projects was increased
from Rs. 1,018 crores to Rs. 1,481 crores, the share
of total outlays declined to 30.8 per cent. But in
spite of only a 45 per cent increase in planned public outlays, Indian economic planners envisaged a
proportionately larger increase in agricultural production during the second plan. Although production
during these years continued to experience annual
fluctuations, the target of 80 million tons was
achieved by 1961.

Planned public outlays on agriculture, community
development, irrigation, and related electric power
projects during the third plan were placed at Rs.
2,730 crores, comprising 37 per cent of total outlays.
The output of food grains was expected to rise by 32
per cent and other crops by 31 per cent.[16] Table 17
indicates the growth of major agricultural commodities in India since 1950.

In spite of the growth of the agricultural sector, its contribution to India's total national income experienced a small but steady decline. This
has been due, in part, to the fluctuations in agricultural production and, in part, to the more rapid
rate of growth of the other sectors of the economy.
In 1950-51, agricultural production comprised 49 per
cent of the country's national income. By 1960-61,
its contribution had declined to 46 per cent. During these years, the agricultural sector grew at an
average annual rate of 2.4 per cent while industrial
production expanded at an average rate of 3.5 per
cent; commerce, transportation, and communication,
3.7 per cent; and the other sectors, 4.5 per cent.

Development of Industry

A major goal of India's industrialization program is to reduce the heavy dependence upon agriculture, as well as to rectify the imbalance between

TABLE 17

Agricultural Production During India's Five-Year Plans

(Units in millions)

	1950-51 Production	First Plan Goal	1955-56 Production	Second Plan Goal	1960-61 Production	Third Plan Goal	1964-65 Production
Food grains (tons)	50.8	61.6	66.8	80.5	82.0	100.0	88.4
Major oilseeds (tons)	5.2	5.5	5.7	7.5	6.9	9.8	8.6
Sugar cane (tons)*	5.7	6.3	6.1	7.8	11.1	10.0	12.3
Cotton (bales)	2.9	4.3	3.9	6.5	5.3	7.0	5.4
Jute (bales)	3.3	5.4	4.2	5.5	4.1	6.2	6.1
Tea (pounds)	607.0	..	665.0	700.0	725.0	900.0	859.0

*Gur only.

Source: Review of the First Five Year Plan, p. 99; Economic Survey 1965-66, Table 1.1.

the consumer goods and heavy industries. In the
IPC's words:

> Low or static standards of living,
> underemployment, and unemployment
> . . . are all manifestations of the
> basic underdevelopment which charac-
> terises an economy depending mainly
> on agriculture. Rapid industrialisa-
> tion and diversification of the econ-
> omy is thus the core of development.[17]

Under the impetus of the development program,
India has experienced a large measure of industrial
growth. The General Index of Industrial Production
indicates an increase of 84 per cent in the volume
of industrial output since 1956.

Industrial production increased rapidly during
the first plan, increasing at an average annual rate
of 5.8 per cent. Between 1956-58, however, production rose only 3.5 per cent annually, or about 60
per cent of the rate of the previous five years.
The setback in the rate of industrial expansion was
due, mainly, to two factors. First, rapidly deplet-
ing foreign-exchange reserves necessitated institut-
ing drastic import restrictions on essential raw
materials, machinery, and equipment which curtailed
expansion of many enterprises. Second, there was a
sharp decline in agricultural production which resulted in a drop in total income. This, in turn,
brought about a decline in demand for certain commodities, particularly cotton textiles. In 1959,
however, industrial production increased sharply,
rising 8.1 per cent over 1958.

The first plan allocated Rs. 176 crores for the
industrial sector, about 8 per cent of total planned
public expenditures. Actual outlays, however,
reached only Rs. 74 crores. Although planned production goals were considered to be relatively modest, their fulfillment was achieved in only a few
industries. Production of iron and steel, for example, fell substantially below planned targets.

Table 18 indicates the volume of production and
planned goals of major commodities during India's
five-year plans.

The second plan shifted emphasis from agriculture to industry and mining, and overwhelmingly to
the development of the production of capital goods.
Public outlays for industry rose from 7.6 per cent
to 18.5 per cent of planned total expenditures.
Industry's share increased to 22.6 per cent after
the revision in 1958. Production of major industrial goods fell considerably below the second plan's
goals. The fall was due in part to the import restrictions imposed in 1957 and 1958. Particularly significant were the relatively poor results achieved in
the iron and steel and cement industries. India's
plans for self-sufficiency in various types of capital goods largely depend upon the achievement of
the goals set for such basic industries.

Whereas the second plan emphasized the expansion of capacity in the iron and steel industry, the
third plan placed emphasis on the development of
basic capital and producer-goods industries, particularly machine building. The third plan's goal was
to build as rapidly as possible sufficient industrial capacity to supply most other sectors of the
economy with machinery and equipment produced in
India. Planned public outlays allocated to industry and mining totaled Rs. 1,520 crores, almost double that budgeted during the second plan.

Other Major Sectors

Among the other sectors of the Indian economy,
sizable sums have been invested in transportation,
communication, and electric power facilities. Expenditures on transportation and communication facilities during the first plan were devoted largely to
the rehabilitation and modernization of existing facilities, particularly railroad installations and
rolling stock. Planned outlays were set at Rs. 570
crores but actual expenditures during the first plan
totaled only Rs. 523 crores.

TABLE 18

Industrial Production and Plans During India's Five-Year Plans,
Selected Major Commodities

	Production 1950-51	First Plan Goals	Production 1955-56	Second Plan Goals	Production 1960-61	Third Plan Goals	Production 1964-65
Finished steel (million tons)	1.0	1.6	1.3	4.3	2.2	6.9	4.4
Pig iron (million tons)	1.6	2.8	1.8	7.5	4.2	...	6.7
Aluminum (thousand tons)	4.0	12.0	7.3	25.0	18.5	75.0	54.1
Cement (million tons)	2.7	4.8	4.6	13.0	8.5	13.0	9.4
Ammonium sulphate (million tons)	0.1	0.5	0.4	1.4	0.4	1.4	0.4
Cotton manufactures:							
Yarn (billion lbs.)	1.2	1.6	1.6	1.9	1.7	2.2	2.0
Cloth (billion yards)	3.7	4.7	5.1	5.4	5.0	5.8	5.2
Sugar (million tons)	1.1	1.5	1.9	2.2	2.4	3.0	3.3
Jute manufactures (million tons)	0.8	1.2	1.0	1.1	1.1	1.2	1.3
Iron ore (million tons)	3.0	...	4.3	12.5	11.0	32.0	15.1
Coal (million tons)	32.8	...	39.0	60.0	55.5	97.0	64.4

Source: Review of the First Five Year Plan, pp. 16-18; Economic Survey 1960-61, Table I.6; Economic Survey 1965-66, Table 1.6; Far Eastern Economic Review, February 4, 1969, p. 263; August 24, 1961, p. 361.

Public outlays on transportation and communication facilities during the second plan were expected to account for 28 per cent of total public expenditures, compared with 24 per cent for the first plan. About 65 per cent of the total allocated was to be spent on the railway system. Although a large part again was allocated for rehabilitation, the emphasis shifted to expansion of existing facilities. Although planned public outlays in this sector during the third plan increased 14 per cent, as a portion of total outlays this sector's share dropped sharply. This has taken place in spite of the IPC's recognition of a "severe shortage of transportation facilities which is expected to continue for some time."[18]

Plans for the development of electric power facilities called for capacity to increase from 2.3 million kw. in 1951 to 9.3 million kw. in 1966. During the first plan, installed capacity was increased to 3.4 million kw., compared with a target of 3.7 million kw. India invested a total of Rs. 302 crores in this sector during the period. Installed capacity was increased further during the second plan to 5.7 million kw., but still fell short of the target of 6.9 million kw. Outlays for this expansion totaled Rs. 525 crores, of which the public sector accounted for Rs. 460 crores.

In spite of the sizable shortfalls during the first two plans, the IPC anticipated an increase in generating capacity of 7 million kw. during the third plan, an annual increase in capacity of about 25 per cent, compared with 14 per cent during the second plan. Expenditures were set at Rs. 1,089.

FINANCING ECONOMIC DEVELOPMENT

India's large-scale development program has placed a heavy strain on its financial resources. Taxation as a source of funds has increased and foreign economic aid has assumed a key role in the development program. Large public outlays for economic development, coupled with heavy defense requirements, have resulted in continuing budget deficits.

These deficits have largely been met by deficit financing which, in turn, has given rise to inflationary pressures.

Investment Plans

In defining its investment plans the IPC has
stated:

> The investments planned for each sec-
> tor represent the best judgment as to
> the amounts needed to achieve Plan
> targets, and to bring about the desired
> balanced development of large and small
> industry and industry and agriculture.[19]

The fulfillment of the goals of India's development
program over the next decade depends largely upon
the economy's ability to provide sufficient resources for a continually increasing volume of investment.

When the first plan was formulated, it was expected that gross domestic investment in India would
rise from 5 per cent of national income in 1950-51
to about 20 per cent by 1968-69. This increase was
subsequently considered to be high and was reduced
to a more gradual increase. The revised targets envisaged a level of investment equal to 14 per cent
of national income by 1965-66 and a maximum of 17
per cent by 1975-76.[20] Aggregate investment during
the first plan totaled Rs. 3,360 crores, slightly
less than planned outlays. The public sector accounted for Rs. 1,800 crores. Investment in the
private sector was channeled largely into construction and agriculture.[21]

Aggregate investment during the second plan totaled Rs. 6,831 crores, an increase of 103 per cent
over the level of investment achieved in the first
plan. Whereas the private sector accounted for 54
per cent of total investment during the first plan,
its share fell to 45 per cent during the second
plan. Moreover, the public sector accounted for the
predominant share of total investment in large-scale

industry, mining, and transportation and communication facilities.

The third plan envisaged investment expenditures totaling Rs. 10,400 crores, an increase of 52 per cent over the level of outlays during the second plan. The more rapid rate of growth planned for the public sector was reflected in the allocation of aggregate investment. During the second plan, investment in the public and private sectors increased 139 per cent and 72 per cent, respectively, over the first plan. The third plan called for an additional 69 per cent increase in the public sector but for only 32 per cent in the private sector. Table 19 outlines total investment expenditures during the three plans.

TABLE 19

Aggregate Investment Expenditures During
India's Five-Year Plans

	First Plan	Second Plan	Third Plan (Planned)	Per Cent Increase	
				Second over First	Third over Second
Public investment	1,560	3,731	6,300	134	42
Private investment	1,800	3,100	4,100	72	32
Total investment	3,369	6,831	10,400	101	54

Source: Tata Industries Private Limited, Statistical Outline of India 1964 (Bombay: Popular Prakashan, 1964), p. 90.

Savings

The ability of India to finance an increasing
proportion of its development program out of its own
resources depends on its ability to mobilize an increasing amount of domestic savings. The IPC originally envisaged an increase in net domestic savings
from about 5 per cent of national income to 7 per
cent during the first plan. By the end of the second and third plans, savings were expected to rise
to 9.7 per cent and 11 per cent, respectively, of
national income. But the fluctuations in the level
of agricultural production, the political obligation
to increase consumption, and the inability to reach
national income goals have made it unlikely that savings will, in the near future, grow at the rate
hoped for by the IPC.

The goal for 1955-56 was exceeded as savings
rose to 9.7 per cent of national income during the
first year of the second plan. The setback in agricultural production in 1957-58, however, reversed
this trend and the rate of savings has remained at
this level since that time. Table 20 indicates the
volume and pattern of savings in India.

Sources of Finance--the Public Sector

The major sources of funds used by the Indian
Government to finance outlays in the public sector
are tax revenues, public loans, deficit financing,
and external assistance. Table 21 details these
sources of funds. The current budgetary resources
available for financing public outlays consist of
the balance from current revenues (at rates of taxation existing prior to the start of each plan) and
revenue from additional taxation introduced during
the course of each plan. Taxation includes excise
and customs duties and income taxes.

Although these tax sources should provide the
bulk of domestic funds for development, their contribution declined during the second plan. Moreover,
planned receipts from these sources have continued to

TABLE 20

Volume and Pattern of Savings in India*

(In crores of rupees)

	1951-52	1955-56	1956-57	1960-61	1961-62	1962-63
Government sector	170.1	117.0	172.0	215.5	312.1	356.0
Domestic corporate sector	58.1	63.1	56.9	96.1	86.3	90.8
Household sector	254.4	839.1	818.3	923.8	813.6	853.9
Totals	483.2	1,019.2	1,047.2	1,235.2	1,212.2	1,300.1
Savings as a per cent of national income	5.3	9.7	9.5	9.7	9.3	9.7

*In 1948-49 prices.

Source: Government of India, India 1965 (Delhi: Ministry of Information and Broadcasting, 1965), p. 163.

TABLE 21

Sources of Funds for the Public Sector's Outlays
During India's Five-Year Plans
(In crores of rupees)

	First Plan		Second Plan		Third Plan	
	Resources Used	Per Cent of Total	Resources Used	Per Cent of Total	Target	Per Cent of Total
Balance from current) tax revenue) Additional taxation)	630	32	1,063	22	2,260	30
Contribution of the railways	122	6	167	3	100	1
Public enterprises' surplus	*	..	*	..	275	4
Public loans	205	10	772**	16	800	11
Small savings	240	12	406	9	600	8
Other capital receipts	155	9	261	5	715	9
Deficit financing	420	21	954	21	550	7
External assistance	188	10	1,049***	24	2,200	30
Totals	1,960	100	4,672	100	7,500	100

*Included under current revenues and miscellaneous capital receipts.

**Includes investment by the State Bank out of P.L. 480 funds.

***This includes investment of P.L. 480 funds by the Reserve Bank in special securities in 1960-61.

Source: Review of the First Five Year Plan, p. 35; Statistical Outline of India 1964, p. 99.

be below expectations as current government expenditures outside the plans have risen more rapidly than
current revenues. Although the second plan's target
for additional taxation was substantially exceeded,
the balance available from current revenues showed a
net decline.[22]

The third plan envisaged an increase of 125 per
cent in tax revenues, rising to Rs. 1,710 crores.
This increase was predicated on the prospect that
national income would increase more than 5 per cent
per annum. The IPC did not indicate how this was to
be achieved but merely stated that the details of
any tax measures adopted "will have to be decided
upon in the light of the emerging economic situation."[23]

Another important source of domestic financing
has been the sale of long-term government securities,
which accounted for 10 per cent of total public outlays during the first plan. The part financed from
this source during the second plan increased to 17
per cent, when revenues from public loans exceeded
the original target by 11 per cent. One of the more
important reasons for this achievement was the treatment of the proceeds of P.L. 480 sales. These funds
were deposited in the State Bank of India and subsequently invested in treasury bills and other government securities.[24]

Another significant domestic source of funds
has been deficit financing, having contributed 21
per cent of total financial resources used during
the first two plans. In spite of the heavy dependence on this source of funds the third plan envisaged a decline in such financing to 7 per cent of
the total funds used. In any comparison, however,
the role of P.L. 480 funds should be borne in mind.
Estimates for the third plan placed all proceeds received from the sale of P.L. 480 commodities under
"external assistance." In second plan figures, only
those P.L. 480 proceeds actually used were considered under external assistance, the balance being
included under deficit financing.

The third plan's original projection was based on what the IPC considered to be a permissible addition to the money supply. The IPC stated:

> On the basis of an estimated quantum of money supply by the end of the second plan, the additional money creation permissible in the Third Plan period might be of the order of Rs. 950 crores--if it is assumed that money supply and aggregate output would be approximately in balance at the end of the second plan. Part of the increase in money supply comes about through the banking system. Allowing for this, the amount of budgetary deficits that could be considered permissible for the Third Plan period is taken at Rs. 550 crores.[25]

One of the major obstacles which India's development program has faced has been the lack of adequate foreign-exchange reserves to finance the required imports. During the first plan, the deficit in the balance-of-payments totaled Rs. 318 crores. Of the total, Rs. 196 crores was financed by external assistance and Rs. 122 crores by drawing on foreign-exchange reserves.

When the second plan was launched, the IPC forecast a trade deficit of Rs. 1,375 crores and a balance-of-payments deficit of Rs. 1,120 crores during those years. The bulk of the deficits were expected to occur during the first three years of the second plan and subsequently decline as imports declined while exports continued to increase. Money drawn from foreign-exchange reserves was expected to total about Rs. 200 crores. But the second plan's greater emphasis on capital-intensive undertakings, plus a substantial rise in the domestic price level, negated these estimates. Imports exceeded expectations in both price and volume, while exports failed to follow the anticipated trend and were lower in 1960-61 than at the beginning of the

second plan. As a result, India experienced consistent and substantial deficits in her balance-of-
payments, which over the five years of the second
plan totaled Rs. 2,059 crores. Money drawn from
foreign-exchange reserves in 1956-57 alone exceeded
the IPC's estimates for the entire second plan.

As India's foreign-exchange reserves dropped
sharply, foreign economic assistance assumed a crucial role in efforts to maintain the tempo of development activities. Whereas external assistance
accounted for only 10 per cent of the total financial resources used during the first plan, it represented 24 per cent during the second plan, rising
from Rs. 188 crores to Rs. 1,090 crores. The IPC
estimated that foreign sources would account for
30 per cent of total financial resources used during
the third plan. During the first four years of the
third plan, foreign aid had already accounted for
33 per cent of total investment. The industrial
sector is particularly dependent upon this source
of financing; foreign economic assistance accounted
for 58 per cent of the total investment in industry
during the second plan.

By the end of September, 1965, Rs. 5,455 crores
($11.4 billion at the official rate of exchange) had
been extended to India in the form of loans, credits, and grants. Of the total, the U.S. accounted
for 54 per cent and the U.S.S.R. and the IBRD 9 per
cent each. Table 22 presents the sources of foreign
assistance during the three plans. The importance
of such aid is reflected in the portion of the
balance-of-payments deficits financed with it.
Whereas foreign economic assistance financed about
29 per cent of the deficit in 1956-57, in the last
year of the second plan it financed about 89 per
cent and covered 68 per cent of the total deficit
for the second plan. In contrast, the IPC originally estimated that external assistance would have to
cover only 35 per cent of the deficit incurred during the third plan.

TABLE 22

External Assistance Authorized and Used for India's Development Plans

(In crores of rupees)

	First Plan		Second Plan		Third Plan	
	Authorized	Utilized	Authorized	Utilized	Authorized (through Sept. 30, 1965)	Utilized
United States	246.3	165.8	1,542.5	812.0	1,138.9	1,507.8
U.S.S.R.	64.7	.	319.0	72.2	100.5	190.6
IBRD	57.7	33.8	265.3	222.6	147.4	112.4
West Germany	.	.	141.4	126.6	276.9	195.5
United Kingdom	.	.	122.6	121.8	213.3	140.9
Colombo Plan	45.5	25.3	61.8	71.0	54.1	43.1
Japan	.	.	35.4	16.0	138.1	83.3
Italy	.	.	.	.	81.3	11.5
Others	0.7	0.7	61.4	17.2	340.6	177.9
Totals	414.9	225.7	2,549.4	1,459.4	2,491.1	2,303.0

Source: Economic Survey 1965-66, Tables 7.1-7.4.

Sources of Finance--the Private Sector

Since the public and private sectors compete
with each other for available funds for investment,
it generally is government policy which determines
how the funds are distributed. The amount of funds
invested annually by domestic private enterprise can
only be estimated because of the fragmentary information concerning the distribution and financing of
such investment in India. Only a small part of the
total savings utilized in this sector passes through
institutional agencies. Most savings are invested
directly by the small farmer or entrepreneur. Moreover, there is much "nonmonetized" investment which
does not enter the national accounts in any form.

Although the private sector fulfilled its
planned investment goals during the first two plans,
the share financed out of its own resources declined.
During the first plan, private sources comprised 74
per cent of total investment but declined to 63 per
cent in the second plan. Capital raised from India's
limited capital market accounted for only 11 per
cent of total private investment in both plans.
Indian officials estimated that almost half of total private investment requirements for the third
plan (including expenditures of Rs. 200 crores on
modernization and replacement) would be financed
from internal resources and about one-quarter from
external assistance.

Financial information is most complete for the
industrial sector, mainly the larger enterprises.
Table 23 details these sources of funds for the private sector.

Private Foreign Investment

In spite of its preference for public investment, India continues to utilize foreign investment
as an important source of capital for economic development. India's fundamental approach to foreign investment is embodied in the late Prime Minister

TABLE 23

Financing Private Industrial Investment
in India's Development Program

(In crores of rupees)

	First Plan	Second Plan Planned	Second Plan Estimated Expenditures	Third Plan Estimates
Private domestic capital				
New issues	40	80	120	200
Corporate profits & reserves	150	300)	400	600
Other sources	61-64	80)		
Capital from govt. or govt.-financed agencies				
Loans from Industrial Finance Corp., State Finance Corp., & Industrial Credit & Investment Corp.	18	40)		
Resources from the National Industrial Development Corp.	. .	55)	80	130
Direct loans, indirect loans, & state participation	26	20	20	20
Foreign capital				
Foreign capital including suppliers' credit	42-45	100	200	300
Totals	337-343	675	825	1,250

Source: The New India, p. 144; Third Five Year
Plan, A Draft Outline, p. 222; Statistical Outline
of India 1964, p. 102.

Nehru's statement of April 6, 1949. Nehru stated:

> The object of our regulation should
> . . . be the utilization of foreign
> capital in a manner most advantageous
> to the country. Indian capital needs
> to be supplemented by foreign capital
> not only because our national savings
> will not be enough . . . but also be-
> cause in many cases scientific, tech-
> nical and industrial knowledge and
> capital equipment can best be secured
> along with foreign capital.[26]

The activities of private foreign investment
are largely governed by the policies set forth in
the Industrial Policy Resolution of 1956. Generally, foreign enterprise is treated much the same as
is private domestic investment. In spite of per-
sistent foreign-exchange difficulties, the government has continued to permit the transfer abroad of
profits, dividends, and interest earned by foreign
investors. The volume of foreign private capital
flowing into India in recent years has averaged
about $100 million annually.

The greater part of foreign investment in India
generally has been directed toward such enterprises
as petroleum processing and marketing, tea planta-
tions, and certain manufacturing activities, e.g.,
tobacco and iron and steel products. Between mid-
1948 and the end of 1958, the value of these investments more than doubled, and by the end of 1961 totaled 580.4 million rupees.[27]

Although the government has permitted foreign
investors to operate in certain industries originally reserved for the public sector, various considerations tend to limit the growth of foreign investment.
The continued growth of public investment in accordance with the Industrial Policy Resolution of 1956
itself tends to narrow the immediate field for private investment. Furthermore, the capacity being

developed by the public sector in such industries as petroleum, iron and steel, and pharmaceuticals tends to place private firms in these industries at a competitive disadvantage. The squeeze is even tighter as a result of the government's obligation to control prices and restrict profit margins. To this must be added the reluctance that stems from the prospects of devaluation, foreign-exchange crises, and political instability.

PATTERN OF U.S. AND U.S.S.R. ECONOMIC AID TO INDIA

In view of the importance of India's viability to the Free World, the industrial countries of the West are underwriting a large part of the foreign-exchange costs of the development program. By far the largest share of this commitment has been financed by the U.S. Through its economic aid program, the U.S. has been an important supplement to domestic savings for investment in India. It also has enabled India to ease the effects of its balance-of-payments problems.

But the U.S.S.R. also is providing substantial amounts of economic assistance for India's economic development. Soviet aid has become one of the most important foreign sources of capital for India's industrial sector. The economic aid being provided by the U.S. and the U.S.S.R. presents a paradoxical situation. Committed as it is to the perpetuation of free enterprise, the U.S. must wrestle with the dilemma of assisting in the development of a "socialist pattern of society." Such aid provides assistance for the avowed Soviet objective of expanding India's public sector. On the other hand, Soviet economic aid, by providing India with needed capital, facilitates India's plans to achieve its development goals within the framework of a free and democratic society.

Magnitude and Character of U.S. Aid

By the end of June, 1965, the U.S. had extended
economic aid to India totaling $6,318 million. In
addition, P.L. 480 sales have generated local currency amounting to some $3 billion. Funds totaling
about $5.2 billion were expended on all U.S. aid ac-
tivities by the end of June, 1965, in addition to an
equivalent of $1.3 billion in P.L. 480 currency.
Table 24 outlines the major types of U.S. aid extended to India.

Indo-American Technical
Cooperation Program

U.S. program assistance to India began on a
small scale in 1951 under the terms of the Point
Four General Agreement concluded on December 28,
1950, subsequently incorporated into the Indo-
American Technical Cooperation Agreement of January 5,
1952. Under the latter agreement, a special organization, the Indo-American Technical Cooperation Program (IATCP), was established to undertake jointly
financed projects in agriculture, industry, transportation, public health, and community development.
The U.S. contribution to this program has consisted
largely of technical services, training of Indian
personnel, materials and equipment (primarily railroad equipment), steel for industrial and agricultural purposes, and fertilizers. The government of
India generally has been responsible for the rupee
expenditures connected with procurement of property,
construction, inland transportation and handling
charges, local costs of U.S. technicians, and salaries of Indian trainees.[28] The counterpart funds
which result from the import of goods for this program are credited to a special development account.

By the end of June, 1963, the last year for
which information was available, expenditures for
IATCP projects had totaled $495 million. The bulk
of these funds was allocated for agricultural, industrial, transportation, and public health programs.
About $68 million of total outlays represented im-
ports of wheat and cotton under the Mutual Security

TABLE 24

U.S. Economic Aid Extended to India,
FY 1946-FY 1965
(In millions of dollars)

	Total	1946-50	1951-61	1962-65
AID and predecessor agencies	2,485	..	1,021	1,464
P.L. 480	3,111	..	1,718	1,393
Title I	2,860		1,569	1,291
Title II	23		6	17
Title III	228		143	85
Wheat Loan of 1951	190	..	190	..
Export-Import Bank	406	..	245	161
Other economic aid	126	39	81	6
Totals	6,318	39	3,255	3,024

Source: U.S. Overseas Loans and Grants.

Act of 1954 (P.L. 665). The rupees generated by
these imports (Rs. 31.9 crores) were deposited to
the account of the U.S. Of this total, Rs. 19.2
crores were loaned to India and Rs. 12.7 crores were
provided as grants.

Wheat Loan of 1951

On June 15, 1951, the India Emergency Food Aid
Act was passed which provided India with a loan of
$189.6 million to purchase about 2 million tons of
wheat in order to avert a threatened famine. The
original terms of the loan called for payments to be
made in dollars over a period of thirty years, beginning on June 30, 1957. In September, 1958, however, the U.S. agreed to revise the payment schedule
to help India alleviate the foreign-exchange crisis.
All principal and interest payments due between the
end of 1958 and mid-1967 were deferred until after
June 30, 1986, and a new terminal date set at June 30,
1995. No interest is being charged on the deferred
installments.[29]

P.L. 480

As of June 30, 1965, agreements totaling $2.9
billion under Title I of P.L. 480 had been concluded
between India and the U.S. Cereals and cereal products accounted for 87 per cent of total agricultural
commodities imported. Cotton comprised the bulk of
the balance with tobacco, dairy products, and fats
and oils accounting for the remainder. The rupee
equivalent of the dollar costs of these imports was
deposited in the U.S. Government Title Account in
India. About 80 per cent of these funds has been
made available to India as loans and grants. The
balance has been retained by the U.S., partly for
its own use and partly for loans to private firms
for investment in India.

Loan and grant allocation of rupee funds totaled $2.3 billion, of which $1.3 billion had been
disbursed by the end of 1964. The part represented
by loans is repayable over a period of forty years

in semiannual installments. Until 1964, the rate of
interest charged on these loans was 4 per cent but
subsequently was dropped to 0.75 per cent. Loans
with options to pay in dollars or local currency carry interest charges ranging between 3-5 per cent.
The period for repayment of local-currency loans to
the private sector averages nine years, with interest
charges ranging between 6-8 per cent.[30]

Additional quantities of surplus agricultural
commodities have been supplied to India through
other arrangements provided for in P.L. 480. Under
Title II, emergency relief assistance authorized for
India amounted to $21.9 million by June 30, 1965.
During the same period, $229 million worth of com-
modities was supplied through nonprofit voluntary organizations under Title III.

Development Loan Fund

AID loans dispensed by the Development Loan
Fund (DLF) through fiscal year 1965 totaled $1.9
billion. Of this total, $1.6 billion had been dis-
bursed. Initially, such loans were of importance
not only for the capital goods provided but also because of the option to repay in Indian rupees deposited in India. Since 1961, AID has required DLF
loans to be repaid in dollars, but the period of repayment has been extended.

Export-Import Bank

Loans from the Export-Import Bank to finance a
variety of development projects totaled $406 million
by mid-1965. Of the total authorized, about $300
million was extended to the Indian Government. Two
large loans totaling $200 million were provided for
general economic development. Actual disbursements
on all loans amounted to $302 million by mid-1965.

Other Types of Economic Assistance

During 1959-60, the U.S. made available to India
foreign currencies equivalent to $6 million for com-
modity imports. This amount of U.S.-owned currencies in Italy, France, and Japan was used to import

fertilizers and tube-well equipment. The rupee
equivalent of these currencies was paid into the
U.S. account in India.

Under an agreement concluded on June 30, 1958,
India received a loan of $20 million for the devel-
opment of the Orissa iron ore mines from the U.S.-
financed Asian Economic Development Fund. The loan
is to be repaid in rupees over a period of fifteen
years beginning three years after disbursements are
made. The rate of interest charged on the loan is
3.5 per cent.

Magnitude and Character of U.S.S.R. Aid

Economic aid extended to India by the U.S.S.R.
totaled $1,022 million by the end of 1965. Other
Communist countries had provided an additional $230
million. Almost all of this aid is being used for
industrial development. The only nonindustrial aid
and the only grants were extended for the construction of two technological institutes and an experi-
mental farm. The total cost of these three projects
is $2.7 million.

Prior to 1955, India's economic relations with
the Communist countries were confined to trade. In
September, 1954, the U.S.S.R. expressed its willingness to assist India in constructing a steel mill
and subsequently sent a survey team to India to select a site for the mill and to prepare a feasibil-
ity study. On February 2, 1955, an agreement was
signed to construct a steel mill at Bhilai with an
annual capacity of 1 million tons of ingot steel.
Although the U.S.S.R. provided credits totaling
$132.3 million to cover the major part of the foreign-
exchange costs of the project, by the time the steel
mill was completed in 1960 the amount of Soviet financial assistance required had risen to $135.9
million.

Nearly three years elapsed before the U.S.S.R.
was to provide additional aid for India's development program. Between November, 1957, and February,

1961, the U.S.S.R. extended credits to India totaling $670 million, largely for use during India's
third plan. Following the Soviet lead, Rumania,
Czechoslovakia, and Poland also provided credits
totaling $90 million. Subsequent Soviet aid exten-
sions to India amounted to about $216 million, al-
most all to finance the first stage of the Bokaro
steel mill. Other East European credits totaled
$140 million.

The Soviet Role in India's
Industrialization

The extent of Soviet participation in India's
industrialization program, particularly during the
third plan, has been extensive. Such assistance has
been particularly important for the construction of
facilities to produce heavy electrical and machine-
building equipment, development of the petroleum industry, and expansion of steel and coal production
and thermal electric power capacity. The machine-
building plant the U.S.S.R. is constructing at
Ranchi with a capacity of 80,000 tons will provide
the bulk of the equipment required for the expansion
of India's steel industry. The foundry forge plant
being built by Czechoslovakia will provide the forg-
ings and castings for the machine-building plant.[31]
Some of the more important facilities being constructed with Soviet assistance are presented in
Table 25.

Soviet activities in the petroleum industry
were begun during the second plan and dominated petroleum development in India's public sector. The
U.S.S.R., with Rumanian participation, provided
India with exploration and drilling equipment and
technical assistance required for exploration.
India contracted for the services of about 100 Soviet technicians to explore for oil.[32] The U.S.S.R.
and Rumania also constructed the only state-owned
petroleum refineries in India. The Soviet refinery
at Barauni and the Rumanian refinery at Nunmati have
a combined annual capacity of 2.7 million tons.[33]

TABLE 25

Major Projects Included Under Indo-Soviet
Economic Aid Agreements

(In millions of dollars)

Year of Agreement	Amount of Aid	Projects
1955	135.9	Bhilai steel mill
1957	125.0	Machine-building plant, Ranchi Coal mining machinery plant and optical glass factory, Durgapur Thermal power plant, Neyveli
1959	20.0	Pharmaceutical plants
1959	375.0	Expansion of plant at Ranchi Expansion of steel mill at Bhilai Expansion of coal mining machinery plant at Durgapur Expansion of thermal power plant at Neyveli Heavy electrical equipment plant at Ranipur Thermal power station, Korba Thermal power station, Obra Precision instruments plant, Kotah Petroleum exploration
1961	125.0	Hydroelectric station, Bhakra Oil refinery, Koyali Coal washery, Kathara Oil and natural gas prospecting
1964	211.0	Bokaro steel mill

Source: "Ten Years of Soviet-Indian Economic
Co-operation," Eastern Economist, February 19, 1965,
p. viii.

The pharmaceutical industry is another in which
the private sector has been predominant but where
the government is expanding its activities with Soviet assistance. In 1956, a team of Soviet and Indian experts conducted a study of the industry in
India and recommended a vast expansion of domestic
capacity utilizing Soviet assistance. Particularly
significant was a statement of an Indian member of
the team who said:

> To use this aid, to the best advantage,
> we must also eliminate the private prof-
> it motive out of the drug industry.
> Profits in the drug industry are . . .
> probably the highest of all industries.[34]

Soviet assistance for Indian agriculture is confined to a $1.8 million mechanized farm in Suratgarh.
This assistance was provided as a grant and is a
display of Soviet-style state farm techniques. The
U.S.S.R. provided the agricultural equipment and
technical services of agricultural specialists. The
project was designed to reclaim 30,000 acres of the
Rajasthan Desert for the production of pedigree
seeds of various varieties of wheat, barley, cotton,
sugar cane, and oilseeds. Acreage also is being devoted to livestock breeding and to the production of
citrus fruits.

Repayment of Soviet Economic Aid

Most of the Soviet credits extended to India require repayment to be made in twelve annual installments beginning one year after delivery of all machinery and equipment for any project. The rate of
interest charged is 2.5 per cent. Payment of the
costs of technical services used for the Bhilai
steel mill is on similar terms.   All Soviet credits
require payments to be made in rupees into a special
account which may be used for the purchase of Indian
commodities or converted into sterling. In September, 1959, an Indian official announced that the
U.S.S.R. had agreed not to insist on sterling but to
accept only rupees.

Indian officials, however, do not consider such repayment terms as being much more advantageous than sterling payments. These officials claim:

> All payments to foreign concerns,
> whether made in rupees in India or in
> foreign currencies abroad, are pay-
> ments in foreign exchange. If the
> rupees are not converted into a for-
> eign currency directly the foreign sup-
> plier will utilize these rupees for
> financing exports from India. In
> either case, India will be losing the
> foreign exchange which India will
> otherwise have earned for supplying
> these goods.[35]

This, of course, assumes that India can always find markets for its exports.

ASSESSMENT AND IMPACT

Economic Aid and Investment

The economic assistance provided to India by the U.S. and the U.S.S.R. has differed not only in magnitude but also in areas of concentration. U.S. assistance has been provided for all sectors of the Indian economy. However, the largest share of U.S. aid has consisted of agricultural commodities and general imports. U.S. technical assistance has touched rapidly upon large numbers of Indian nationals in all fields of activity, from public health and education to multipurpose projects and transportation.

Soviet aid, on the other hand, is almost completely concentrated on industrial development in the public sector. Soviet projects are generally identifiable as Soviet undertakings and appeal to India's fervent aspiration for industrialization.

U.S. aid expenditures have been an important supplement to domestic savings in India. Assuming that the agricultural commodities imported under the aid program enabled India to import an equivalent amount of investment goods, then U.S. outlays comprised 16 per cent of total investment in India during the first two plans. Furthermore, such aid equalled 30 per cent of total investment in the public sector. Table 26 presents Indian investment and U.S. aid expenditures through the fourth year of the third plan.

Soviet expenditures totaled about $158 million during the second plan, mainly for the construction of the Bhilai steel mill, and $157 million during the first four years of the third plan. These expenditures represented about 9 per cent of total foreign aid outlays in India and about 15 per cent of such assistance used in the industrial sector. Total Soviet expenditures accounted for less than 5 per cent of total industrial investment during these years.

Continuing Need for P.L. 480 Assistance

P.L. 480 assistance requirements are likely to remain at a high level during the next few years. Such aid has continued to increase in spite of the general expansion of foodgrain production. The rising population and growth of per capita income resulted in an increase in demand which has outdistanced the growth in domestic production. Imports of food grains totaled 1.1 million tons in 1956, jumped to 3.6 million tons in 1960, and have fluctuated between 3 million tons and 5 million tons since that time. The greater part of these imports represented P.L. 480 commodity assistance.

Assistance provided to India under the P.L. 480 program has had two important advantages. First, the availability of U.S. agricultural commodities enabled India to import a larger volume of such commodities without additional drawing on scarce foreign-exchange reserves and permitted an increasing level of per capita consumption of cereals,

TABLE 26

Investment and U.S. Economic Aid During India's Development Plans,*
1951-52 Through 1964-65

(In millions of dollars)

	Total Investment	Public Investment	U.S. Aid Expenditures	U.S. Aid as a Per Cent of Total Investment	U.S. Aid as a Per Cent of Public Investment
Agriculture & community development	5,096	2,045)	1,081	11	17
Irrigation & electric power	4,633	4,408)			
Industry & mining	8,551	3,930	565	7	14
Transportation & communication	5,970	4,936	541	9	11
Social services & miscellaneous	10,581	3,198	271	2	8
Other			3,111**		
Totals	34,831	18,517	5,569	16	30

*Partly estimated.   **Largely P.L. 480 imports.
Source: Third Five Year Plan, p. 59; Statistical Outline of India 1964,
p. 97; Statement of Loans and Authorized Credits, pp. 12-15, Status of Loans as
of December 31, 1965; Economic Survey 1965-66.

a politically desirable objective in itself. The foreign exchange conserved was then ostensibly available
for the import of capital goods. Second, the subsequent availability of rupee accounts provided a
source of budget support without having to create
money equal to those accounts. Moreover, this addition to the supplies of food tended to lessen the
inflationary impact of increased consumer demand
stimulated by the expansion of economic activity.

Economic Aid and the Public Sector

For the most part, U.S. aid to India has flowed
to the public sector. Such aid has increased the resources of the public sector relative to the private sector and has enabled the government to pursue
policies which have tended to restrict the activities of private investment and have discouraged a
larger inflow of foreign private capital. It is
estimated that by the end of 1960 only about 10 per
cent of total foreign aid provided to India was received by the private sector.[36]

It is not possible to determine the precise distribution of U.S. aid between the public and private
sectors, but several examples may serve to illustrate
the pattern of aid flow. By the end of fiscal year
1965, about 95 per cent of AID loans were received
by the public sector. Less than 10 per cent of P.L.
480 currencies programmed through 1964 were allocated for use in the private sector. About 25 per
cent of Export-Import Bank loans were directly allocated to private firms.

This observation was highlighted with some concern in the Comptroller General's review of the U.S.
aid program to India. The report states:

> One of the objectives of the United
> States aid to India is to give encour-
> agement to the private sector of the
> economy and strengthen the role of
> private enterprise. To adequately
> meet this objective has given some

concern to responsible United States
officials because India has relied
heavily on government initiative and
financing within the framework of its
5-year plans. . . . The bulk of
United States aid went for state supported and directed projects.[37]

The U.S.S.R. has been more successful in direct-
ing its aid in channels consistent with its objectives. Soviet expenditures during the second plan
accounted for nearly 20 per cent of public investment in the industrial sector and Soviet assistance
available when the third plan was begun represented
almost one-fourth of total planned public investment
in industry.

Aside from the philosophical question of the
desirability of an expanding state sector, there are
the practical economic and foreign policy considerations. Perhaps the most important question from the
standpoint of economic aid is the use of such aid.
Certainly, the U.S. must have some reasonable assurance that the resources provided India through our
economic assistance are being employed as effectively
as possible. On balance, it may be assumed that
state-directed activities generally are not nearly
as efficient as those in the private sector. The
fact that many investment decisions in India, e.g.,
location of a plant, often are based on political
considerations is itself a factor which tends to
lower the efficiency of the investment. It is at
this point, however, that the over-all objectives of
U.S. foreign policy become important considerations.

The Incremental Capital-Output
Ratio Pitfall

The size of planned investment and, consequently, foreign aid requirements for India's development
program rest heavily on the estimated yield from
new investment as represented by the incremental
capital-output ratio. Indian economic planners
originally assumed that for the ten years beginning

in 1951 this ratio would be 3 to 1. After that period, the ratio was expected to rise gradually to
4 to 1 by 1970 and to continue at that rate after
1970.

Although there was a shortfall in actual outlays during the first plan, the favorable results
achieved indicated a capital-output ratio of 1.8:1
and led Indian planners to revise optimistically
future anticipated yields from investment. A
capital-output ratio of 2.3:1 was estimated for the
second plan and 2.6, 3.4, and 3.7 for the third,
fourth, and fifth plans, respectively.[38] The revision of these ratios indicated that Indian officials
believed that the underlying conditions of the first
plan would continue to prevail. Much of the increase in agricultural production, however, resulted
from two consecutive years of favorable monsoons--
a natural phenomenon which did not occur during the
second plan. Moreover, the relatively low ratio for
the first plan also was affected by the sizable un-
used capacity in agriculture which can be used only
during years of favorable monsoon rains.

Also contributing to the lower ratio was the
relatively large nonmonetary investment in the agricultural sector. Such investment usually is in the
form of direct employment of labor and materials in
digging wells, constructing small buildings, and
undertaking other improvements. Investment of this
kind takes place continually but is not included in
plan estimates of investment. The size of this investment has not been quantified but it has been
estimated at about Rs. 1 billion annually.[39]

The anticipated increase in the incremental
capital-output ratio allowed for the planned increase in industrial investment but the 2.3: 1 ratio
for the second plan was too optimistic. Wilfred
Malenbaum has pointed out that historical experience
indicates that a ratio closer to 3.5:1 would be more
appropriate.[40] Results of the second plan, in fact,
indicated a ratio of 3.4:1. In view of the capital
intensive nature of the third plan, the estimated
2.6:1 is even more unrealistic.

In determining the capital-output ratio for India, the IPC has applied capital coefficient data applicable to industrialized countries. Within the framework of India's social and economic structure, the use of coefficients employed in the U.S., Japan, or the U.S.S.R. is not particularly relevant. Moreover, ratios for different sectors will vary considerably. For the U.S., for which sectoral figures probably are the most complete, the highest sectoral coefficient was 100 times as high as the lowest one.[41]

Notes to Chapter 4

1. Radharani Choudhury, The Plans for Economic Development of India (Calcutta: Bookland Private, Ltd., 1959), p. 51.

2. Ibid., p. 64.

3. Government of India, The New India (New York: The Macmillan Company, 1958), p. 66.

4. Deendayal Upadhyaya, The Two Plans: Promises, Performance, Prospects (Lucknow: Rashtradharma Prakashan, Ltd., 1958), p. 35.

5. Government of India, Second Five Year Plan (New Delhi: Planning Commission, 1956), p. 22.

6. Ibid.

7. D. R. Gadgil, Planning and Economic Policy in India (Poona: Gokhale Institute of Politics and Economics, 1961), p. 28.

8. Celia I. Herman, Investment in India, U.S. Department of Commerce (Washington: 1961), p. 196.

9. Government of India, First Five Year Plan (Delhi: Planning Commission, 1953), p. 15.

10.   Government of India, _India 1961_ (Delhi: Ministry of Information and Broadcasting, 1961), p. 187.

11.   _The New India_, p. 23.

12.   Herman, _op. cit._, p. 78.

13.   Government of India, _Selected Plan Statistics_ (New Delhi: Planning Commission, 1959), p. 18.

14.   Government of India, _Third Five Year Plan, A Draft Outline_ (New Delhi: Planning Commission, 1960), p. 10.

15.   _Ibid._, p. 11.

16.   Government of India, _Third Five Year Plan_ (New Delhi: Planning Commission, 1961), p. 61.

17.   _Second Five Year Plan_, p. 25.

18.   _Third Five Year Plan_, p. 540.

19.   _The New India_, p. 130.

20.   _Second Five Year Plan_, p. 10.

21.   Aggregate investment figures for the private sector can only be estimated and represent primarily monetized investment. Substantial sums are invested in agriculture, small industrial enterprises and trades, and transportation for which no figures are available. Rough estimates from sample surveys suggest that 20-25 per cent of all investment (about 50 per cent of rural investment) was nonmonetized in the preplan years.   (Wilfred Malenbaum, _East and West in India's Development_ [Washington: National Planning Association, 1959], p. 25.)

22.   _Third Five Year Plan_, p. 95.

23.   _Third Five Year Plan, A Draft Outline_, p. 50.

24. The aggregate figure obscures a misleading aspect of this category. The IPC made no distinction between government securities purchased by individuals and nonbanking institutions and securities absorbed by the banking system. Subscriptions of the banks to the open-market sales of government securities lead to an expansion of credit facilities and might properly be placed in the same category as deficit financing. Nonbank purchases represent a genuine withdrawal of purchasing power. The amount purchased by the banking system is difficult to determine but it appears to be sizable. One author points out that during the first three years of the second plan, the total value of government securities sold on the open market totaled Rs. 542 crores. In the same period the banks increased their holdings of government securities by Rs. 241 crores. (I. S. Gulati, Resource Prospects of the Third Five Year Plan [Bombay: Orient Longmans Private, Ltd., 1960], p. 40.)

25. Third Five Year Plan, A Draft Outline, p. 49.

26. Quoted in Herman, op. cit., p. 195.

27. Michael Kidron, Foreign Investments in India (London: Oxford University Press, 1965), p. 187.

28. Government of India, External Assistance 1961 (New Delhi: Ministry of Finance, 1962), pp. 3-4.

29. Ibid., p. 15.

30. AID, Status of Loan Agreements as of December 31, 1965 (Washington: 1966).

31. Third Five Year Plan, A Draft Outline, p. 213.

32. Far Eastern Review, February 4, 1960, p. 243.

33. The New York Times, June 17, 1960, p. 5.

34. S. S. Sokhey, The Indian Drug Industry and its Future (New Delhi: New Age Printing Press, 1959), p. 2.

35. M. A. Master, "External Assistance for the Five Year Plans," The Asian Economic Review, III (May, 1961), 216.

36. Ibid., p. 223.

37. The Comptroller General of the United States, Examination of Economic and Technical Assistance Program for India, Fiscal Years, 1955-1958, Report to the Congress of the United States (Washington: 1959), p. 25.

38. Second Five Year Plan, p. 8.

39. N. A. Sarma, "Economic Development in India: The First and Second Five Year Plans," International Monetary Fund Staff Paper, VI (April, 1958), 209.

40. Malenbaum, op. cit., p. 15.

41. Benjamin Higgins, Economic Development (New York: W. W. Norton and Company, 1959), p. 645.

CHAPTER **5** UNITED ARAB REPUBLIC:
PREDOMINANCE OF
SOVIET ECONOMIC AID

Egyptian economic policy in recent decades has
been concerned primarily with maintaining a balance
between the growth of the domestic product and the
more rapid increase in the Egyptian population.
Compared with the period between 1880 and 1914, the
years of Egypt's most rapid economic growth, the
decades since World War I have witnessed a sharp decline in the rate of growth of the Egyptian economy.
During this period, the costs of agricultural production rose as the use of chemical fertilizers increased substantially and greater use was made of
marginal areas. Meanwhile, the Egyptian economy was
squeezed by an extended period of depressed conditions in the cotton market: first by a decline in
the price of cotton during the 1920's and then by
the worldwide depression of the 1930's.

While the rate of economic growth in Egypt declined, the rate of population growth experienced an
upward and accelerating trend and currently is increasing at 2.9 per cent annually. This combination
of a declining economic rate of growth and a rapid
population increase precipitated a sharp decline in
per capita income. One author estimates that the net
income of the Egyptian peasant in 1913 prices declined from LE 13.5 in 1913 to LE 7.5 in 1951, a
decline of 44 per cent.[1] The effect of the population increase on Egypt's meager resources also is
dramatically reflected in the pressure on the land.
In spite of an increase in cropped area from 7.9
million acres in 1912 to 9.5 million acres in 1948,
the ratio of population to cropped area declined
from 0.64 to 0.48.[2]

120

THE DEMISE OF THE TRADITIONAL SOCIETY

On July 24, 1952, the Farouk dynasty was over-
thrown by a military coup and the foundation was established for a violent upheaval in Egypt's traditional
social and economic structure. The impending radical changes, however, were not immediately discern-
ible. In the early months of the Neguib regime, the
government followed generally conservative economic
policies, the primary aim being to create an atmosphere of confidence for private, especially foreign,
capital.[3] But the uncertainty concerning the stability of the new government and its future political and economic policies did little to create that
atmosphere. Moreover, the conflict with the British
over the Suez Canal added to the reluctance of the
international business community to invest in Egypt.

On March 28, 1954, Neguib was ousted and Gamal
Nasser emerged as the most powerful individual in
Egypt. Whereas Neguib's stated intention was to
hold elections and return the government to civilian
control, Nasser postponed the elections and insti-
tuted an authoritarian military regime. Neguib had
sought to eliminate the abuses existent in Egypt, but
to preserve the society of which he was a product.
Nasser and the Free Officers who engineered the coup
had no such ties to the monarchical system in Egypt,
which found its support among the wealthy landowners,
industrialists, and merchants.[4] In fact, it was
these groups of which Nasser was suspicious and
whose power he subsequently destroyed. Speaking at
a rally commemorating the ninth anniversary of the
overthrow of the monarchy, Nasser stated:

> It was obvious, from the first day of
> the Revolution, that our objectives
> could not be realized until our society
> was completely and permanently liber-
> ated from all forms of exploitation.
> That was abundantly clear on July 23,
> 1952, and it was one of the basic prin-
> ciples of this revolution.

> We, the July 23 Revolution, do not
> correct. We make a complete change
> . . . we must change society complete-
> ly, from its base. We must build a
> new society the foundations of which
> conform to our aspirations and what we
> fought for. We should build a new
> State.[5]

Filling the "Power Vacuum" in the Middle East

The domestic and foreign policies followed by the U.A.R. since 1954 generally have reflected Nasser's aspirations, philosophy, and ambitions. There would appear to be little doubt that Nasser was concerned with conditions in Egypt and that he was determined to lift the masses from their poverty, industrialize and modernize the Egyptian economy, eliminate the stagnation of Egyptian society, and remove the foreign political influences existent in Egypt. But this search for dignity soon developed an anti-Western character and Nasser's subsequent obsession with the elimination of Western influence from the Middle East soon deterred him from concentrating Egypt's energies on the country's real problems.

On July 27, 1954, agreement was reached for evacuation of British troops from the Canal Zone, ending seventy-two years of British occupation. But the relatively friendly relations between Egypt and the West engendered by the treaty were short lived. On February 24, 1955, Iraq joined in a military alliance with Turkey, a treaty which formed the basis for the Baghdad Pact. Iraq's action was taken in the face of Arab, primarily Egyptian, opposition and brought to the fore the traditional Iraqi-Egyptian conflict for dominance in the Arab world. Following close on the heels of this political setback for Egypt, on February 28, 1955, Israeli commandos launched a large-scale attack into the Gaza strip. Both events had their effect on Egyptian policy for they highlighted Egypt's military weakness vis-à-vis Iraq and Israel.

Nasser, pressed and frustrated by these events which threatened the existence of his regime, looked for the support he could not expect to find in the West. He found a willing ally in the U.S.S.R., which also was engaged in violent attacks against the Baghdad Pact and only recently had initiated its post-Stalin policy to cultivate the nationalist regimes emerging among the developing countries. On September 28, 1955, Nasser announced the conclusion of a $250 million arms agreement with Czechoslovakia.[6] The agreement, hailed in the Arab world as a blow to colonialism, projected the U.S.S.R. into the Middle East as a champion of Arab nationalism and catapulted Nasser to a position as its unchallenged leader.

The arms agreement set off a chain reaction of events which witnessed the cancellation of a joint U.S.-U.K.-IBRD offer to finance the construction of the Aswan High Dam, Egyptian retaliatory nationalization of the Suez Canal, and the launching of a punitive attack on Egypt by Israel, France, and the U.K. Throughout this period Nasser's prestige in the Arab world continued to rise, reaching its zenith with the Egyptian-Syrian union on February 21, 1958, which formed the United Arab Republic.

Although the Arabs have blamed the West for Nasser's decision to turn to the Communist countries for arms, it appears that "positive neutralism" already had evolved as a cornerstone of Egyptian foreign policy and the purchase of Soviet arms may well have been the first manifestation of this new policy. One author has claimed that the arms agreement was, in fact, the earliest expression of Egyptian independence and neutrality, implying that military equipment might not have been purchased from the West even if available. The author states:

> Once the British evacuated Suez, Egypt
> was free to express its independence
> through neutrality. . . . This, in con-
> junction with Israeli military behaviour,
> led to the Russian-Czechoslovak deal of

1955. This was not just another trade
agreement. . . . The agreement stressed
Egypt's independence, and was instru-
mental in making Egyptian leadership
acceptable to most Arabs.[7]

GROWTH OF THE STATE SECTOR

Perhaps the most significant change which the
Egyptian economy has undergone since 1952 has been
the growth of state participation in the country's
economic activities. During the early months after
July, 1952, the government gave little indication
that an omnipresent public sector eventually would
emerge. Even the most radical of the regime's policies at that time, agrarian reform, was not designed
to catapult the state into widespread involvement in
the Egyptian economy. In addition to destroying the
traditional power structure in Egypt, agrarian reform served to attack an institution which kept the
Egyptian peasantry impoverished.

Nearly two-thirds of Egypt's arable land was
owned by 6 per cent of the landowners, while more
than 94 per cent existed on five feddans or less.[8]
The combination of increasing demand for arable land
and limited possibilities for increasing the availability of that land generally maintained the price
of land at an inflated level. High prices resulted
in high rents which, in turn, absorbed most of the
small landowners' income. The inability to accumulate savings necessitated borrowing at high rates
of interest to maintain the cultivator during the
growing season. Consequently, the peasant was
caught in the vicious circle of his own poverty.

In September, 1952, a comprehensive Land Reform
Law was promulgated which limited ownership of land
holdings to 200 acres per owner. A subsequent de-
cree of July 25, 1961, reduced to 100 acres the area
which could be owned by one individual. Under the
original law the landowner received an indemnity for
the requisitioned portion of his land equivalent to

ten times the rental value of the land, including
any capital investments added. The indemnity is
paid in 3 per cent government bonds redeemable in
thirty years. The land requisitioned is distributed among farmers owning less than five acres,
each recipient being allotted an area of two to five
acres. The cost of land to the farmer is equal to
the amount of indemnity paid by the government plus
15 per cent for expenses. The land originally was
purchased from the government on a thirty-year credit with interest at 3 per cent.[9] Under an amendment
introduced in 1958, the repayment period was extended
to forty years, while the rate of interest was low-
ered to 1.5 per cent and administrative charges to
10 per cent.

In January, 1953, a National Production Council
(NPC) was created, establishing the first Egyptian
organization concerned with centralized economic
planning responsibilities. The NPC was authorized
to draft plans and establish priorities in economic
development and empowered to carry out projects
either through the regular ministries or through independent organizations established for specific
undertakings.[10] As the government slowly increased
its participation in developmental projects, the
level of public investment increased. Prior to
1952, the amount of public expenditures on economic
development was relatively small compared with investment in the private sector. But the volume of
private investment subsequently experienced a rapid
decline while that of the public sector jumped sharply. In 1955, public investment exceeded the volume
of private outlays. This trend is represented in
Table 27.

The events of the latter half of 1956 triggered
the actions which have since profoundly altered
Egypt's economic and social structure. During the
several years that followed, the administrative apparatus of the state organization blossomed forth
and the stage was set for the eventual socialization
of much of Egyptian economic activity. A variety of
government-controlled companies were created with

interests in all sectors of the Egyptian economy.
Some were established to manage the foreign-owned
assets expropriated after 1956.

TABLE 27

Total Gross Investment in Egypt,
1950-56

(In millions of pounds)

	1950	1951	1952	1953	1954	1955	1956
Total investment	115	143	116	116	135	122	110
Gross private investment	112	103	83	64	57	54	39
Public investment	22	29	25	34	53	62	66
Change in stocks	-19	11	8	18	25	6	5

Source: Economic Developments in the Middle
East 1956-1957, p. 13.

Once nationalization was set in motion, the regime employed such policies with increasing frequen-
cy, often to achieve political as well as economic
objectives. Although nationalization measures resulted in a more equitable distribution of national
income, placed much of the country's productive assets in the hands of the state, and channeled the
country's financial resources into state-directed investments, Nasser also used the state apparatus to
destroy Egypt's traditional economic structure and
change its political character. Private investment
in Egypt was represented by the small groups of

wealthy Egyptian landowners, industrialists, and financiers who maintained close contacts with foreign capital. Nasser viewed both domestic and foreign capitalists as the traditional exploiters of the Egyptian masses and considered the elimination of their influence as essential before real economic and social progress could be achieved.

In the years since 1956, the area left to private investment has been narrowly circumscribed and all new private investment must be adapted to the goals of the development plan. Foreign trade is completely nationalized, as are the press and most wholesale distribution activities. All banks and insurance companies in the U.A.R. were nationalized, enabling the government to divert domestic funds from agriculture, real estate, and the stock market to investment in the industrial sector.

It is in the industrial sector, however, where the growth of government activity has been most extensive. Whereas ownership and operation of industrial enterprise were largely functions of private interests, the government now is responsible for the major share of investment and controls numerous concerns through the corporate structure it has created. Most of the government's activity in the industrial sector is the responsibility of the Economic Development Organization (EDO), a government corporation established on January 13, 1957. The EDO is responsible for coordinating all government investment activities and is endowed with broad powers to establish commercial, financial, industrial, agricultural, and real estate companies. By 1960, the EDO owned varying shares in the capital stock of 57 companies with capital assets totaling LE 506 million.[11]

In spite of the large volume of investment required for the development program, the government has shown little desire to attract foreign private capital. In fact, Nasser has made it quite clear that he prefers government-to-government credits and loans and is unwilling to accept foreign private investment.[12] Between 1956 and 1960, there was a net outflow of foreign private capital from the U.A.R.

totaling LE 28.6 million. Earnings of foreign enterprises transferred to countries of origin declined from LE 3.8 million in 1956 to LE 225,000 in
1959. At the end of 1960, there were only 100 foreign companies with a total capital investment of
LE 20 million still operating in the U.A.R.[13] The
continuing nationalization of privately owned investments since 1960 has further reduced the size of
these investments.

The year 1961 probably was the most critical in
the centralization process. July, 1961, is hailed
as "a month of destiny" in which "traditional rela-
tionships in all spheres of economic and social existence have been either eliminated or have undergone far-reaching and basic changes."[14] Sweeping
nationalization measures placed in the hands of the
public sector all foreign trade, about 90 per cent
of industry, all financial institutions, and a substantial portion of internal trade and transportation. In addition, a highly progressive income tax
was introduced, an individual's annual company earnings were limited to LE 5,000, employees and workers
of privately owned enterprises were required to receive 25 per cent of the establishment's net distributed profits, and the amount of land holdings
permitted was further limited.

The sundering of the Egyptian-Syrian union in
September, 1961, spelled the final blow to large-
scale Egyptian private enterprise. The political
rupture again brought to the fore Nasser's suspicion
of the Egyptian entrepreneurial class, and he vented
his wrath on it. Within a few days a large number
of Egyptians were arrested and the property of several hundred others seized in retaliation against
"capitalists and reactionaries who persisted in taking advantage of all classes of people for their
own interests."[15] By this time, Nasser could truly
state: "Brothers, citizens . . . is there anything
left. . . . We have so far nationalized every-
thing."[16]

GROWTH OF THE NATIONAL PRODUCT

Data pertaining to the growth of the Egyptian economy are not precise and are often contradictory. The U.N. estimates that real national income increased about 3-4 per cent annually during the 1950's.[17] U.N. statistics, however, indicate that between 1953 and 1961, national income in current prices nearly doubled, rising from LE 780 million to LE 1,482 million, or an annual increase of 5.9 per cent. Table 28 presents the data related to the growth of the Egyptian national product from 1950 through 1961.

TABLE 28

Growth of Egyptian National Product

	Net National Product*	National Income	Population (millions)	Per Capita Income
	(In millions of Egyptian pounds)			
1953	. .	780	22.0	35.4
1954	. .	868	22.6	38.4
1955	925	900	23.1	38.9
1956	951	913	23.6	38.7
1957	979	1,085	24.2	44.8
1958	1,100	1,188	24.8	47.9
1959	1,210	1,324	25.4	52.1
1960	1,275	1,420	25.9	54.4
1961	1,320	1,482	26.7	55.4

*At 1954 prices.

Source: U.N., Statistics of National Income and Expenditure, p. 85; Monthly Bulletin of Statistics, May, 1966, pp. 171, 179.

TABLE 29

Development Projects of the National
Production Council
(In millions of pounds)

Sector and Project	Total Estimated Cost	Budget Appropriations 1953/54-1955/56	Expenditures to June 30, 1955
Agriculture	99.4	52.6	39.9
Irrigation & drainage	42.2	22.5	10.8
Land reclamation	12.4	12.4	4.0
Pumping stations	28.1	7.8	20.9*
Miscellaneous projects	16.8	10.0	4.3
Electric Power	43.1	33.0**	20.7**
Aswan Dam	27.5	21.2	14.2
Cairo power stations	15.6	11.8	6.5
Transportation & communication	65.3	35.0	13.2
Railways	23.4	8.1	4.6
Telecommunication	19.4	5.7	3.6
Highways	11.9	14.5	3.9
Other	10.5	7.6	1.1
Industry	40.5	6.3	0.7
Aswan fertilizer plant	22.0	2.1	0.1
Helwan iron & steel plant	16.0	1.5	0.3

TABLE 29 (continued)

Sector and Project	Total Estimated Cost	Budget Appropriations 1953/54-1955/56	Expenditures to June 30, 1955
Industry (continued)			
Suez petroleum refinery	2.5	2.6	0.3
Miscellaneous	2.5	5.3	2.1
Totals	250.8	132.1	76.7

*Including an estimated LE 15.1 million spent before 1953-54.

**Including LE 11.8 million spent prior to 1953-54.

Source: Economic Developments in the Middle East 1954-1955, pp. 114-15.

Development of Agriculture

In 1953, the government formulated a two-phase program to increase the area under cultivation by almost 50 per cent. The short-term program expected to reclaim an area of 607,000 acres.[20] The long-term phase centers around the construction of the Aswan High Dam. Between 1953 and 1956, LE 25.6 million were spent for agricultural development projects.[21] Various schemes were undertaken to reclaim 610,000 acres by 1956. The Liberation Province scheme to reclaim 208,000 acres was launched in 1954, but by the end of 1959 only 17,200 acres actually had been reclaimed and cultivated.

Since 1950, the contribution of agriculture to the Egyptian national product has declined steadily. In 1956, agriculture accounted for 33 per cent of national income, compared with 44 per cent in 1950. In 1963, this sector's share of national income rose from about 15 per cent to 23 per cent. The share of national income represented by government activities increased from 12 per cent to 17 per cent.

EGYPTIAN ECONOMIC DEVELOPMENT
PRIOR TO 1959

Postwar Public Development

By the end of World War II, Egyptian economic growth no longer could keep pace with the growth of population. Although Egyptian officials directed some of their efforts toward stimulating economic development, they were not generally effective and accomplishments fell considerably short of desired goals. Between 1945 and 1951, public expenditures for economic development, mainly in the agricultural sector, totaled LE 128 million.[18] The result of all agricultural programs during this period was to expand the area under cultivation by only 162,000 acres.

In 1953, the NPC formulated a program calling for the expenditures of LE 132 million during the three-year period 1953-54 to 1955-56 on a variety of development projects, including several started prior to 1953. Details of the development plan are presented in Table 29. By the end of June, 1958, LE 146 million had been spent on these projects. The sums earmarked for public expenditures for development projects in the six budgets covering the period 1952-53 to 1957-58 totaled LE 1,716 million.[19]

The production of most of the U.A.R.'s major
crops experienced a moderate degree of expansion after 1950, largely from the increased use of chemical
fertilizers. The area devoted to the two major
crops, cotton and wheat, remained relatively stable
but output was increased. Production of cotton
increased from about 8.9 million metric tons in 1952
to about 9.6 million metric tons in 1960. Wheat
production rose from 1.1 million metric tons to 1.5
million metric tons during the same period.[22] The
production of rice nearly tripled during these
years, largely as a result of an increase in the
area devoted to this crop.

Development of Industry

In 1957, Egyptian officials formulated a five-
year industrialization plan as the first stage of a
program by which it was expected that national income would be doubled in twenty years. In view of
an anticipated rise in the Egyptian population of
about 8 million during that period, the government
considered it necessary to raise national income
from LE 900 million to LE 2,470 million.[23] During
this first stage, Egyptian officials envisaged a
total investment of LE 250 million in the industrial
sector. Of this total, manufacturing and processing
industries were allocated LE 162 million; expansion
of the petroleum and mining industries, LE 56 million; expansion of the petroleum and mining industries, LE 56 million; technical training, LE 2.5
million; and reserves, LE 20 million.[24] Many of the
projects included were begun prior to the formulation of the plan. No formal investment program for
the other sectors was announced.

The industrialization plan was launched in
1958, but was hardly a year old when the government
announced that the investment program not only would
be completed in 1960, but that total planned investment would reach LE 330 million.[25] Furthermore, the
time period for doubling national income was reduced
to ten years. By the end of 1959, eighty-six projects valued at LE 85.9 million were completed. The

iron and steel plant at Helwan accounted for LE 23 million, or 27 per cent of the total value of completed projects. In addition, twenty-three vocational training centers were completed at a cost of LE 2.2 million.

The expansion of industrial production between 1952 and 1959 was relatively large compared with the rate of growth of agriculture, with most of the major industries experiencing substantial growth. The production of cotton manufactures increased almost 100 per cent; raw sugar, 43 per cent; fertilizer, 75 per cent; cement, 87 per cent; and iron and steel products, more than 240 per cent. The value of industrial production rose from LE 680 million to LE 904 million.[26] The index of industrial production in 1959 rose 42.3 per cent over the level of 1952. Production increased 7 per cent in 1957 and 11.5 per cent in 1958, compared with an annual average increase of 4.7 per cent between 1952 and 1956. The growth of industrial production is indicated in Table 30.

The relatively steady growth of Egyptian industry prior to 1958 was stimulated, for the most part, by the government's policy of encouraging domestic investment in industry. Excise taxes and foreign-exchange controls were imposed on imports which competed with domestically manufactured goods, while imports of raw materials and machinery required for local industry entered free of duty. Tax exemptions were granted to new enterprises during the first years of operation and credit facilities were provided through the Industrial Bank. In some of the major enterprises, the government participated by furnishing a large share of the capital.

Among the major industries in which sizable investments were undertaken were fertilizer, iron and steel, and petroleum. Expansion of the fertilizer industry was designed to meet agriculture's increasing demand for chemical fertilizers. In spite of an increase of 75 per cent in domestic production between 1952 and 1959, however, imports of chemical fertilizers increased 51 per cent.

TABLE 30

Index of Industrial Production in Egypt,
1952-59

(1954 = 100)

	1952	1953	1954	1955	1956	1957	1958	1959
General index	95.0	96.7	100.0	110.0	115.1	123.7	137.3	141.5
Processing of agricultural commodities	145.3	129.2	100.0	134.8	105.6	132.1	154.5	166.6
Mining and quarrying	118.3	111.5	100.0	103.6	95.8	117.6	153.3	154.0
Manufacturing	91.8	93.6	100.0	109.4	117.2	123.4	134.1	137.8
Electricity	50.7	96.8	100.0	113.8	124.6	136.5	153.6	171.4

Source: National Bank of Egypt, Economic Bulletin, No. 1, 1961, p. 110.

Egypt's desire to reduce the volume of its imports of iron and steel products led to the construction at Helwan by a West German firm of the first integrated plant in Egypt. The plant was completed in 1958. The plant's operation has been costly and in 1959, when consumption of ingot steel was only 112,000 tons, operated at less than half of total capacity.[27] The ore used by the plant is brought from Aswan by rail; much of it is low in quality and requires concentration before it can be used. Furthermore, all the coke and spare parts for the plant's operation are imported. The extent of the high cost of production was indicated by a Soviet engineer's recommendation in 1960 that production be increased to 210,000 tons and any surplus exported. These exports should then be subsidized to make them competitive by raising the charge to domestic consumers by $5 per ton.[28]

A major effort also was made to expand the production of crude petroleum and refined products to keep pace with the expansion of economic and military requirements. Between 1952 and 1959, the production of crude petroleum rose from 2.6 million tons to 3.3 million tons. The production of refined products also experienced a steady increase, reaching a level of 4.4 million tons in 1960, an increase of 70 per cent.

THE FIRST FIVE-YEAR PLAN

On July 1, 1960, the U.A.R. launched its first five-year plan (July, 1960-June, 1965) as the first of two plans designed to double national income in ten years. The plan envisaged a total investment of LE 1,577 million by which total national output was expected to increase 42 per cent (LE 1,076 million) and national income 40 per cent (LE 513 million).[29] The level of investment was expected to rise from 12.5 per cent of national income to 18.4 per cent.

The largest increases were expected to occur in the industrial sector; production was to increase

by 59 per cent and account for 41 per cent of the
increase in national income. As a result of these
increases, the contribution of the industrial sector to total national income was to rise from 21
per cent to 30 per cent. At the same time, agriculture's share was expected to decline from 31 per
cent to 28 per cent. The agricultural sector was
allocated 23 per cent of total investment but accounted for only 15 per cent and 22 per cent, respectively, of the planned increases in production
and national income.[30] The agricultural sector,
however, was expected to provide larger increases
as the benefits from the Aswan High Dam begin to
accrue after 1965.

Development of Industry

The first five-year plan continued the emphasis
on industry begun in 1958. The allocation of LE 439
million for the development of this sector comprised
about one-quarter of total planned investment. Of
the total investment originally planned for the industrial sector, LE 315 million were allocated for
metallurgical, engineering, petroleum, chemicals,
and mineral development projects. The metallurgical and engineering industries were allocated the
largest share of industrial investment, LE 107.3
million.

Investments planned for the development of the
petroleum and mineral industries totaled LE 119 million. As a result of the investment in this industry, crude oil production was expected to rise to
8.5 million tons by the end of the second plan and
refining capacity from 3.5 million tons to 6.5 million tons. Investments budgeted for the development
of mineral resources envisaged extensive development
of existing mineral deposits, particularly iron ore
and coal. The U.A.R.'s requirements for iron ore
are critical in view of the continuing expansion of
the Helwan iron and steel plant. It was expected
that by mid-1965 domestic requirements of iron ore
would total 1.4 million tons.[31]

Development of Agriculture

In spite of the large-scale plans for industrialization, the agricultural sector still must carry
the overwhelming share of the burden of meeting the
requirements of a rapidly growing population and
provide the means for financing the increased imports of industrial equipment. But any hope of a
large increase in agricultural production ultimately
depends upon a substantial increase in arable land;
Egyptian agriculture already is one of the most intensive in the world. Perennial irrigation and the
extensive use of fertilizers give yields per acre of
many crops which are among the highest in the world.
Current reclamation programs may result in an increase in arable land of about 10 per cent but this
still will not be adequate to meet the country's
rapidly expanding requirements. It is for this reason that the U.A.R. considers construction of the
Aswan High Dam a sine qua non if any increase in
living standards is to be achieved. Area under cultivation might be increased by as much as 50 per
cent by 1970 when the arable land provided by the
dam and its related irrigation facilities is added
to that of other irrigation and reclamation projects.
Planned outlays for agricultural development in the
first plan originally totaled LE 391 million, of
which irrigation and reclamation projects accounted
for LE 292 million.[32]

The Aswan High Dam

The most important single project in the
U.A.R.'s economic development planning is the Aswan
High Dam project (Sadd-El-Aali Project). Upon completion of the dam and related irrigation facilities,
it is anticipated that land available for cultivation will be increased about 30 per cent. After a
preliminary survey undertaken in 1955, the IBRD recommended a project with a total cost estimated at
about $1.3 billion for the construction of two cof-
fer dams, the main dam, seven diversionary tunnels,
related irrigation facilities, and four power sta-
tions. This study envisioned construction which
would be undertaken in two stages and completed in
about ten years. Completion of all hydroelectric
facilities was expected to take an additional five

years.[33] The estimated cost of the project subsequently was revised downward to $1,053 million.
Public expenditures on the project were estimated at
LE 271 million and investment outlays by private
interests at LE 96 million, or 26 per cent of total
expenditures. A distribution of estimated expenditures on the High Dam is presented in Table 31.

TABLE 31

Distribution of Planned Investment in
the Aswan High Dam

	Million Pounds	Million Dollars*
Total investment	367.0	1,053.3
Public investment	271.0	777.8
Dam & civil works	121.5	348.7
Power plant & transmission lines	81.5	233.9
Irrigation & related facilities	58.0	166.5
Service facilities	10.0	28.7
Private investment	96.0	275.5
Development of newly reclaimed land	70.0	200.9
Development of land converted from basin to perennial irrigation	7.0	20.1
Housing	19.0	54.5

*Converted at LE 1 = $2.87.

Source: The Middle East Economist (January,
1960), p. 3.

Extensive economic benefits are expected to result from the completed project. These include:

a) an increase in cultivable land of 1.3 million acres and conversion of 700,000 acres from basin irrigation to perennial irrigation;

b) an improvement in drainage conditions in cultivable areas which may increase agricultural production by about 20 per cent;

c) the elimination of destructive annual flooding;

d) an improvement in the navigability of the Nile;

e) the provision of hydroelectric power potential of about 10 billion kwh, representing a tenfold increase over present consumption of electric power in the U.A.R.;

f) an increase of LE 255 million in national income.[34]

In spite of the substantial increases in arable land and production which will result from the completion of the Aswan High Dam, the pressure of population on the land will remain relatively constant. It is estimated that the Egyptian population will increase 28.4 per cent by 1970. The ratio of arable land to population will increase only from 0.23 to 0.24 and that of crop area to population from 0.38 to 0.42.

Also of importance is the effect on the agricultural population which will result from the mechanization of agriculture. Rural overpopulation in relation to resources has been a serious problem in Egypt for many decades. In 1955, the surplus population was estimated at 5 million people, or 22 per cent of the total Egyptian population.[35] If this proportion is maintained as the population increases, surplus population will rise to 7.4 million by 1970. Although a sizable number of people are expected to

be settled on newly developed land, mechanization
still will add to the size of rural unemployment.
The government's plans for a large expansion of industry are not likely to absorb sufficient numbers
of displaced agricultural workers while at the same
time providing jobs for the growing urban labor
force.

To p 152

FINANCING ECONOMIC DEVELOPMENT

Financing Past Expenditures

The sums spent on development prior to 1960 are
difficult to determine from the fragmentary information available. U.A.R. officials estimated that
gross investment (public and private) between 1950
and 1958 averaged LE 127 million annually. They also
estimated that domestic sources provided approximately 80 per cent of the total amount invested.

Traditionally, the major portion of investment in
Egypt was undertaken by the private sector. Private
investment in industry is estimated to have totaled
LE 86.3 million during the years of 1954-57. Total
private investment in industrial and commercial enterprises increased from LE 235.4 million in 1954 to
LE 343.6 million in 1958.[36] The major private industrial companies, particularly the Misr industries,
financed their expansion primarily from their own
resources. Since 1949, the Industrial Development
Bank has been another, though relatively small,
source of funds. Although larger sums were made
available in subsequent years, the Development Bank
still had provided only LE 1.4 million for investment in industry by the end of 1958.[37] During these
years, the government covered most of the cost of
its developmental outlays with the sale of bonds,
contributions from the regular budget, and with bank
credit.

The extent to which public and private investment was financed with commercial bank credit cannot
be determined, as the material available does not

categorize these credits by end use. The volume of
commercial loans and bills discounted rose from LE
111 million in 1952 to LE 240 million in 1959; about
one-third of these funds normally were used to finance the cotton crop. The sale of government bonds
had become an important source of finance during
this time. But, here too, the government employed a
large part of the funds received for current activities, particularly to finance the purchases of cotton. The public debt increased from LE 258 million
in 1952 to LE 399 million in 1959. The part of the
debt attributed to the sale of treasury bills during
the same period increased from LE 60 million to LE
165 million.

Financing the Development Plans

Since 1957, the government has undertaken to
finance the bulk of investment in the U.A.R. During
the course of the five-year plan, the major share of
planned annual expenditures of LE 339 million was allocated for public projects. Expenditures in the
public sector have been financed largely through a
development budget. Between 1957-58 and 1961-62,
the sums allocated for this budget increased almost
tenfold. Table 32 presents a distribution of these
budgets. After fiscal year 1962, the development
budget was discontinued and its components distributed between the general services budget and the
enterprises budget, largely in the latter budget.
Most of the financing for the budgets has been obtained through domestic taxes, surpluses yielded by
the public enterprises, revenues from government
services, balances of the social insurance and pen-
sion funds, and releases of P.L. 480 funds. The
deficits are covered largely by borrowing from the
banking system.

Total budgetary expenditures increased rapidly
during the first plan. In 1958-59, budgetary outlays for the ordinary, development, and annexed budgets totaled LE 439 million. The combined budgets
for 1961-62 were more than double, having risen to
LE 847 million with the bulk of these funds allocated

for industrial development, social welfare, and defense. The proposed budget for 1964-65 again had
more than doubled, jumping to LE 1,776 million. A
large part of such outlays was financed by borrowing
from the Central Bank.

TABLE 32

Development Budgets of the United Arab Republic,
FY 1958-FY 1962

(In millions of pounds)

	1957-58	1958-58	1959-60	1960-61	1961-62
Agriculture	5.3	8.3	15.6	34.7	40.3
Electric power	4.7	5.2	5.4	9.1	15.3
Mineral development	2.1	1.6	1.5	2.0	..
Communications project	13.9	11.5	11.2	46.6	56.5
High Dam project	2.8	2.6	13.2	16.3	13.7
Other independent organizations	6.1	7.7	4.4	33.0	31.8
Suez Canal	..	..	..*	19.0	18.0
Public utilities	..	..	..*	15.3	10.2
Social services	..	..	..*	27.8	29.2
Five-Year Industrialization Plan	..	12.0	45.5	84.0	93.3
Miscellaneous	..	..	..	..	6.7
Totals	34.9	48.9	96.8	285.8	315.0

*Included in the ordinary budget in 1959-60.

Source: U.A.R., The Budget Report, July 1959-
June 1960 (Cairo: Ministry of Treasury, 1960),
p. 38; The Middle East Economist (August, 1960),
pp. 23-26; (July, 1961), p. 330; Economic Development in the Middle East 1958-1959, p. 120.

U.A.R. economic planners expected to finance a
large part of the development program from a substantial increase in the level of domestic savings.
Between 1960 and 1965, the level of domestic savings
was expected to rise from 11 per cent of national
income to 21 per cent, or LE 141 million to LE 377
million.[38] A rise of this magnitude would have required an annual average increase of 21.8 per cent,
a rate of growth which must be considered optimistic.
By the end of the first plan, the level of savings
totaled about LE 288 million and accounted for about
15 per cent of national income.

In spite of the large degree of dependence upon
domestic borrowing, the Egyptian economy did not experience any significant degree of inflation until
1964. The price level between 1952 and 1964 showed
almost no increase but by mid-1965 it had jumped almost 20 per cent. The price stability which prevailed prior to 1964 was largely due to the extension
of price controls and food subsidies and the government's willingness to channel excess demand toward
imports. These imports, combined with the demands
of the development program, resulted in large import
surpluses and chronically large balance-of-payments
deficits. During the years of 1960-64, the import
surplus totaled nearly $1.7 billion while the deficit
in the balance-of-payments averaged $240 million an-
nually. These deficits were financed largely by
drawing on foreign-exchange reserves and foreign
borrowing. Between 1954 and 1961, reserves declined
from $558 million to $29 million and have remained
at a low level ever since.

An important trend in U.A.R. financing of economic development since 1957 has been the increasing
dependence on foreign loans and credits. In 1960,
the foreign-exchange costs of the plan were expected
to total about $1.6 billion.[39] Because the plan fell
below planned goals, only about $1 billion in loans
and credits was used. About half of such expenditures represented outlays under Communist credits.[40]

RESULTS OF THE FIRST FIVE-YÉAR PLAN

Considering the ambitious nature of the U.A.R.'s development program, it is not surprising that the five-year plan's achievements were well below planned goals. Nevertheless, the accomplishments of the plan compare favorably with growth rates achieved in most other developing countries. The annual increase in national income of about 6.5 per cent was close to the plan's goal of 7 per cent. Per capita income increased about 3.5 per cent as the rate of population growth averaged 2.9 per cent annually rather than the 2.3 per cent originally anticipated. The impact of this increase in income, however, is dulled somewhat by the sharp rise in the price level during the last eighteen months of the plan.

In terms of investment and output the plan's achievements also appear favorable. Table 33 presents some of the results in certain important categories. Actual investment expenditures amounted to 96 per cent of the plan's objective. Since official statistics are in current prices, the ratio, in real terms, is somewhat lower. In the all-important area of production, official statistics show a ratio of achievement of 86 per cent. Nasser, however, has stated that actual achievement was only 81.5 per cent, which may reflect the growth in real terms.[41] The actual growth in national income was about 93 per cent of the planned growth. The key agricultural and industrial sectors, however, were well below the growth planned for these sectors.

U.S. ECONOMIC AID TO THE U.A.R.

Between 1947 and mid-1965, the U.S. extended economic assistance to the U.A.R. totaling $1.2 billion. Although the U.S.S.R. and other Soviet Bloc countries have extended a larger amount of aid, U.S. expenditures far exceeded those of the Communists. The difference lies in the relative characters of the two aid programs. Of the total of U.S. aid extended, about $980 million was in the form of

TABLE 33

Planned and Actual Achievements During the Five-Year Plan

(In millions of pounds)

Sector	Investment		Increase in Production		Increase in National Income	
	Planned	Actual	Planned	Actual	Planned	Actual
Agriculture, including High Dam	391	355	162	88	107	72
Electric power	140	113	111	166	14	13
Industry	439	404	609	392	260	129
Construction	.*	.*	.*	-67**	4	45
Transportation & communication	272	294	29	67	25	62
Housing	175	162	12	14	11	7
Services	160	185	153	221	92	149
Totals	1,577	1,513	1,076	926	513	477

*Included in other categories.

**A sharp decline was registered during the last year of the plan. During the fourth year of the plan, the value of construction was LE 202 million, 50 per cent above 1959-60.

Source: U.A.R., Statistical Pocket-Book of the United Arab Republic 1952-1964 (Cairo: Department of Public Mobilization and Statistics, 1965); U.S. Department of Commerce, JPRS: 34,108, Translations on the Middle East No. 190, February 14, 1966.

P.L. 480 commodities. In addition, AID obligations
totaled $171 million and Export-Import Bank loans,
$48 million. The bulk of these authorizations have
been utilized. In addition, an equivalent of $685
million in local currency generated by P.L. 480 sales
was programmed for use by the U.A.R.

Large-scale economic aid to Egypt was launched
in March, 1953. The Suez crisis of late 1956 brought
a temporary halt to U.S. aid activities and new obligations were not undertaken again until July, 1959.
Since that time, P.L. 480 assistance has been a primary source of Egyptian wheat imports.

The important difference between U.S. and
U.S.S.R. economic aid to the U.A.R. is that little
of American assistance has been directly allocated
for development purposes. Of the total of non-P.L.
480 assistance, about $85 million was obligated for
the industrial sector, $50 million for agriculture,
and $31 million for electric power facilities. Ap-
proximately $48 million was used to purchase trans-
portation equipment. In 1962, two AID loans totaling $30 million were applied to an economic stabi-
lization program.

U.S. assistance for Egyptian agriculture has
consisted largely of the construction of grain storage facilities and a reclamation project. A DLF
loan of $17 million was provided in 1962 for the
grain storage project, but only $1.1 million had
been used by mid-1965. The most important agricultural project undertaken with U.S. assistance was
launched in 1953 with an agreement for the reclamation of 40,000 acres and the undertaking of community development and rural rehabilitation projects
in the governates of Beheira and Fayum. The U.S.
originally contributed $10 million to this program,
and Egypt, $15.6 million.[42] A separate entity to
administer the program, the Egyptian American Rural
Improvement Service (EARIS), was established. In
January, 1959, the U.S. obligated an additional $1.7
million to this program. By the end of 1960, 23,000
acres had been reclaimed and 900 families resettled

on these areas. The original agreement was extended
until 1964 to enable the completion of the reclamation plan for the remaining 17,000 acres.[43]

THE SOVIET AID PROGRAM IN THE U.A.R.

Development of Economic Relations

Egyptian economic relations with the Communist
countries prior to 1955 were limited exclusively to
trade. Postwar trade with these countries reached a
peak in 1948, when it accounted for 11 per cent of
Egypt's total trade. Trade between the two areas
subsequently declined, reaching a low point of 3 per
cent of Egypt's trade; but by 1954 it again accounted
for 10 per cent of total Egyptian trade. The door
to the development of full-scale political and economic relations, however, was not opened until the
conclusion of the arms agreement with Czechoslovakia.

to p. 123

It seems likely, however, that an expansion of
economic relations with the Communist countries was
in the offing even if an arms agreement had not been
concluded with the Communists. In March, 1955, Nasser alluded to the importance of small nations avoiding involvement in the East-West conflict and the
potential advantages to be gained by exploiting this
conflict. Pointing to Egypt's heavy economic dependence on the West and the declining demand for
Egyptian cotton in Western markets existing at that
time, he observed that prospects existed for large
sales in the Soviet Bloc, sales which could be used
to purchase in these countries a large part of the
increasing Egyptian demand for manufactured goods.
Nasser saw this development as a means of balancing
Egypt's economic relations between East and West.[44]

The immediate economic effect of the détente
between Egypt and the U.S.S.R. was a rapid geographic reorientation of Egypt's trade toward the Communist world. In 1955, trade with these countries
comprised 13 per cent of total Egyptian trade but it
rose rapidly until it reached a peak of 40 per cent

in 1958. The most significant development in this
shift in Egypt's trade pattern was the large volume
of cotton--Egypt's chief commodity-source of foreign
exchange--exported to the Communists. During the
cotton-marketing year (September-August) of 1953-54,
cotton shipments to the Communist countries accounted
for 15 per cent of total Egyptian cotton exports but
rose to 66 per cent in the 1958-59 marketing year.
Since that time, these countries have become a relatively stable market for Egyptian cotton, and their
share of total Egyptian cotton exports has not fallen
below 52 per cent. Table 34 presents the growth of
U.A.R.-Soviet Bloc trade since 1953.

The Economic Aid Program

The U.S.S.R. has become the most important foreign participant in the economic development program
of the U.A.R. Since early 1958, the U.S.S.R. and
other Communist countries of the Soviet Bloc have
provided the U.A.R. with economic aid credits totaling $1.5 billion, of which the U.S.S.R. has accounted
for more than $1 billion.[45] About $665 million was
extended for use during the five-year plan. This
economic assistance was available for use in the most
important sectors: $325 million for the multipur-
pose High Dam project; $315 million for industrial
development; and $25 million for municipal and rural
development projects.

The Industrial Sector

The conclusion of the Soviet-Egyptian Economic
and Technical Aid Agreement of January, 1958, immediately enabled the U.S.S.R. to participate exten-
sively in the industrial development plans of the
U.A.R., particularly in the development of mineral
and petroleum resources and metal manufactures.
Originally scheduled for use during the industrialization plan of 1958, the Soviet credit of $175 mil-
lion was incorporated into the five-year plan. The
agreement included a variety of mineral exploration
and development projects; thirty-two metallurgical
engineering, petroleum, and chemical projects; and

TABLE 34

The U.A.R.'s Trade with the Communist Countries

	Total Trade of the U.A.R. (millions of Egyptian pounds)	Total Trade with the Communist Countries	Per Cent of Total U.A.R. Trade	Total Exports of Cotton* (millions of cantars)	Cotton Exports to the Communist Countries	Per Cent of U.A.R. Cotton Exports
1954	299	25	9	5.5	1.5	28
1955	333	49	15	6.5	2.6	39
1956	328	75	23	5.1	2.7	52
1957	355	127	36	5.7	3.6	64
1958	406	152	37	7.3	4.8	66
1959	382	143	37	8.5	4.7	55
1960	430	140	32	7.5	4.8	64
1961	399	131	33	7.1	4.3	60
1962	459	165	36	6.4	3.9	62
1963	625	211	34	6.5	3.4	52
1964	648	222	34	7.6	4.5	59

*Marketing years 1954-55 through 1963-64.

Source: Economic Bulletin, No. 4 (1965), Table 3; Middle East and African Economist (March, 1965), p. 3.

seven food-processing and textile plants.   The
U.S.S.R. also agreed to undertake a major expansion
of the Alexandria shipyard and to establish fifteen
vocational training centers.[46]

In the metallurgical and engineering industries, the agreement called for the construction of
rolling mill facilities at Helwan and iron ore sin-
tering and concentration plants at Aswan. Soviet
engineers recommended the installation of facilities
to produce 300,000 tons of sheets and strips annually
as the minimum required for economic production.[47]
Other projects included in the agreement were plants
to produce nonferrous metal products, welding elec-
trodes, cast iron products, aluminum cables, machine
tools, and surgical instruments.

During the plan, LE 48 million was to have been
invested in seventy-eight projects to expand the capacity of the textile industry. A large part of the
foreign exchange costs of these projects was to have
been financed with credits extended by Soviet Bloc
countries. The Soviet economic aid agreement provided for the construction of three cotton spinning
mills and a plant to produce textile equipment. Two
cotton textile finishing mills, a cotton spinning
mill, and a wool spinning mill were constructed under an economic aid agreement signed with East Germany in 1958. The East Germans also constructed a
100,000 spindle cotton spinning mill, for which a
credit of $8.6 million was extended.[48]

In the petroleum industry, extensive geophysi-
cal surveys and exploration and drilling operations
were undertaken. Much of the equipment for the construction of additional petroleum refining capacity
was covered by the Soviet economic aid agreement,
including the expansion of the government-owned refineries at Suez and Alexandria by 1 million tons
each. The total cost of the projects constructed
with Soviet assistance accounted for about one-third
of total investment originally planned for the
U.A.R.'s petroleum industry.

The Agricultural Sector

The major undertaking by the U.S.S.R. in the agricultural sector is connected with the construction of the High Dam. In addition to supervising the construction of the project, the U.S.S.R. provided a long-term credit of $325 million to finance the foreign-exchange costs of the project. The basic agreement incorporated extensive modifications in the plans prepared by the IBRD. In place of the seven diversionary tunnels, Soviet engineers cut one open channel. Construction of the entire project now is being accomplished in one stage by overlapping the two stages suggested by the IBRD. The two coffer dams and diversion canal were completed in 1964, and it is expected that the main dam and three power units will be completed by 1967.

The financial benefits of the changes introduced by Soviet engineers are not precisely known. The estimate of $1,053 million mentioned above, however, is $118 million less than the IBRD estimate of $1,171 million for the comparable categories of investment. The credit of $325 million extended by the U.S.S.R. to cover the foreign-exchange costs of construction is $32 million less than the IBRD estimate of foreign-exchange costs of the project. This figure approximated an official Egyptian estimate that LE 12 million will be saved by adopting the modifications introduced by Soviet engineers.[49]

Terms of the Major Soviet Agreements

The provisions of the Soviet aid agreements concluded with the U.A.R. are similar to and generally reflect the terms provided other recipients of Soviet aid.[50] These agreements establish lines of credit upon which U.A.R. organizations responsible for implementing planned projects can draw to pay for certain foreign-exchange expenditures. The aid agreements cover the cost of project surveys, preparation of plans and specifications, machinery and equipment for contracted projects, the salaries of Soviet technicians, and the expenses incurred by

Soviet technicians in traveling to and from the
U.A.R.   Pricing of machinery, equipment, and materials purchased from the U.S.S.R. are, according to
the agreements, based on world market prices.

These credits are repaid over a period of
twelve years, commencing one year after completion
of delivery of all machinery and equipment for a
particular plant.   In the case of the High Dam, repayment commenced one year after completion of the
construction of the first stage.   Interest charges
of 2.5 per cent begin to accrue immediately after
the drawing of any part of a credit and are payable
within the first three months of the year following
the year of accrual.   By the end of 1965, the U.A.R.
had paid $15.6 million on the principal and $4 million in interest on the Soviet credits for the High
Dam.[51]

To p 159

The credits were extended in rubles of a specified gold content which placed its value at the
prevailing official rate--4 rubles to $1 prior to
1961 and 1 ruble to $1.111 subsequently.   Repayments
are credited in Egyptian pounds to a special account
in the National Bank of Egypt in favor of the State
Bank of the U.S.S.R.   The credits accumulated in
this account are then used to purchase Egyptian commodities.   In the economic aid agreement, the repayment clause states that the U.S.S.R. may convert its
account payable into sterling or some other convertible currency, implying that the U.S.S.R. has the
option of accepting commodities or convertible currency.   Correspondence appended to the High Dam
agreement, however, may indicate the actual meaning
of this clause.   In the agreement, Soviet importing
organizations are to be granted the prevailing discounts on Egyptian exports provided to hard currency countries.   If, for some reason, such discounts
cannot be granted, or if specified commodities cannot be made available for delivery within six
months, then the account may be converted into convertible currency.   In effect, the U.S.S.R. is in-
sisting that the ruble be considered on a par with
convertible currencies and is able to do this by

exploiting its dominant position as the largest single buyer of the U.A.R.'s cotton.

The agreements obligate the host government to provide Soviet technicians with certain local facilities which are not covered by the credit. These include living accommodations, office space, medical care, interpreters, and, when required, facilities for traveling in the U.A.R. For its part, the U.S.S.R. guarantees that the materials and equipment are as stated in the specifications and that any facilities constructed by it will operate at the required capacity. Machinery and equipment are guaranteed to operate without defect for twelve months or they will be replaced at the expense of the U.S.S.R.

"Socialist Cooperation"

An important technique which the U.S.S.R. has employed to implement economic aid projects in the U.A.R. is to subcontract certain projects to other countries of the Soviet Bloc. In fact, the economic aid agreement specifically states:

> The Government of the U.S.S.R. and the Government of the Republic of Egypt agree that for the execution of this agreement the Soviet party may cooperate with the corresponding organizations of Peoples' Democratic countries in prospecting work, deliveries of equipment, machinery and materials as well as rendering other kinds of technical assistance stipulated under this agreement.[52]

Of the forty-six projects completed under the Soviet agreement, the U.S.S.R. subcontracted five projects to Czechoslovakia, two to Poland, and one each to Bulgaria, East Germany, and Hungary. There also were indications that the U.S.S.R. had subcontracted certain parts of the High Dam project to several of these countries.[53]

IMPACT AND OUTLOOK

The Development Program

On July 1, 1965, the U.A.R. launched its second
development plan. Originally conceived as a five-
year plan, it was rescheduled for implementation
over a seven-year period early in 1966. This plan
envisages a total investment of LE 3,165 million.
Average annual expenditures of LE 452 million are 43
per cent higher than actual outlays during the previous plan. The plan continues the emphasis placed
on industrial development begun in 1958. About 35
per cent (LE 1,102 million) of planned investment is
scheduled for industry, compared with 27 per cent of
actual outlays during the five-year plan. Agriculture has been allocated 19 per cent of planned outlays, in contrast with the 24 per cent of total investment during the previous plan. Development of
transportation and communication facilities accounts for the same share as that spent during the
first plan, 18 per cent.[54]

Although the U.A.R. achieved a relatively favorable rate of economic growth during the five-year
plan, prospects do not appear equally favorable for
a continuation of this rate during the current plan.
The seven-year plan faces economic difficulties much
more serious than those which prevailed five years
earlier. Mobilizing sufficient domestic resources
has become increasingly difficult. Nationalization
of private investment--an important source of such
assets early in the five-year plan--offers little in
the way of meeting these demands. The price increases on goods produced by public-sector enterprises near the end of the previous plan were partly
in response to the government's need to increase financial resources available for investment. And inflation, not a problem in 1960, has become an important consideration as a result of the demands of
the development program.

Contributing significantly to the growing economic difficulties and inflationary pressures are

the U.A.R.'s chronic balance-of-payments deficits.
Government-imposed price increases in 1964 and 1965
were partly designed to curb the import of many consumer goods. The foreign-exchange crisis persists
and is not likely to be alleviated during the course
of the present plan. The need to import foodgrains
remains critical and may not be met by P.L. 480 imports to the same extent as previously. The total-
ity of the country's economic problem is further
compounded by a rapidly growing population, which is
likely to increase at a faster rate as the benefits
of modern hygiene become more widespread.

Growing Dependence on Foreign Aid

As with other developing countries undertaking
large-scale economic development programs, foreign
economic assistance has assumed a critical role in
the U.A.R.'s economic development. During the years
of the five-year plan, the U.A.R. spent LE 410 million from foreign loans and credits received, representing 26 per cent of total investment in the plan.
This aid presumably does not include P.L. 480 commodity imports totaling about $785 million. If it
is assumed that the foreign-exchange conserved was
used for the import of investment goods, then foreign aid expenditures in the U.A.R. were equivalent
to 45 per cent of total investment during the plan.

U.S. outlays, including P.L. 480 expenditures,
during these years totaled about $970 million. Such
expenditures were equivalent to about one-quarter of
U.A.R. investment in the plan. P.L. 480 currency
disbursements accounted for another 5 per cent of
investment outlays.

Aid expenditures by the U.S.S.R. and other Soviet Bloc countries were about half of those of the
U.S., representing about 13 per cent of total U.A.R.
investment. Communist outlays, however, were channeled entirely into specific sectoral projects.
Such assistance accounted for about 25 per cent of
U.A.R. investment in industry, electric power, and
the High Dam. Nearly 45 per cent of total outlays

for the expansion of electric power facilities represented Soviet Bloc aid expenditures.

The availability of Soviet assistance undoubtedly encouraged the formulation of a development plan
well beyond Egyptian financial capabilities. When
the five-year plan was devised, Soviet aid was the
only significant foreign source of financing.[55] It
is certain that in the absence of Soviet aid only a
far less ambitious program would have received support from Western sources. This is particularly
true of the industrial sector where an expanding
public sector would have come into conflict with official Western support for private enterprise. Without an alternative source of capital, such as the
U.S.S.R., it is probable that Nasser would have been
more amenable to a less ambitious program and one
oriented more toward the private sector. By mid-
1965, economic strains induced by an extended period
of Soviet-encouraged economic and military outlays
were sufficient to cause the regime to undertake a
review of its development plan and economic plight
in general and to stretch out the period of its second development plan.

Aid Requirements for the Seven-Year Plan

U.A.R. annual requirements for foreign economic
assistance are likely to be much larger during the
seven-year plan. In a speech delivered on May 1,
1966, Nasser stated that LE 400 million ($920 million
at the official rate of exchange) in foreign aid
would be required for the plan.[56] This estimate
would seem to be highly unrealistic as it approxi-
mates the aid utilized during the previous plan--a
plan in which total investment was half the amount
planned through mid-1972. Moreover, not only will
financial assistance be required to cover the
foreign-exchange costs of the plan, but it is likely
that additional assistance will be necessary to re-
finance some of the existing obligations. And all
of this does not include the kind of aid represented
by P.L. 480.

It is more likely that the U.A.R. will require
at least $1.8 billion in foreign aid to help cover
the foreign-exchange costs of the seven-year plan.
Few commitments for the plan have been obtained from
Western countries. The U.A.R. can no longer count
to any significant degree on the short- and medium-
term loans of foreign banks and firms which provided
significant amounts of funds for the previous plan.
The country's prolonged economic difficulties have
raised questions concerning its creditworthiness.
Political problems have precluded any significant
long-term commitments from the U.S. and West Germany
--the U.A.R.'s most important Western sources of
economic aid.

The Deepening Involvement of the U.S.S.R.

Thus far, the only important foreign aid commit-
ments--more than $1 billion--have been obtained from
the U.S.S.R. and other Soviet Bloc countries. About
$835 million has been extended since 1963, and some
$185 million probably remains available from credits
extended earlier. As a consequence, the U.S.S.R.
will play a much larger role in the U.A.R.'s development program than previously. Communist financing
may account for 20-25 per cent of investment during
the second development plan. What is more important,
such assistance represents 38 per cent of planned
industrial investment. Among the major Soviet undertakings will be an expansion of the Helwan steel
mill's capacity from 300,000 tons annually to 1.5
million tons, and the construction of a lubricating
oil plant with an annual capacity of at least 60,000
tons.[57]

In addition to its aid for the industrial sector, the U.S.S.R. also extended a $67 million credit
in 1964 for the reclamation and development of
210,000 acres of desert land. According to the
agreement, the U.S.S.R. will provide the technical
assistance and all machinery and equipment for the
project.[58] This assistance is in addition to the
area being reclaimed as a result of the construction
of the High Dam.

The Political Determinants
of Economic Aid

Contributing to the exacerbation of the
U.A.R.'s economic difficulties are the regime's external political commitments. In his efforts to
eliminate what he considers to be imperialist influences in the Middle East, to maintain his dominant
position in the area, and to play a vital role in
Afro-Asian affairs, Nasser is pursuing a highly ambitious development program, is overindustrializing,
and is maintaining large military, diplomatic, and
propaganda establishments. He seeks major power influence without major power resources and the economic drain is reflected in the country's economic
difficulties. The development program itself--con-
ducted within the framework of "Arab socialism"--has
political overtones, as one of Nasser's objectives
in this respect is to project an image of the U.A.R.
to be emulated by other Arab states.

In pursuit of his objectives, Nasser has come
into continual conflict with Western interests. As
the U.A.R.'s estrangement from the West has continued, Egyptian dependence on Soviet largesse has increased. Not only has such conflict frequently affected the flow of capital from private and official
Western sources, but the costs of foreign involvement
have grown. Only the U.S.S.R. has been prepared to
finance these costs.

Nasser's experience in accepting Soviet aid
since 1956 without any apparent sacrifice of Egyptian independence has increased his belief in his
ability to continue to do so. While Nasser's primary motivation undoubtedly remains one of strengthening the U.A.R.'s independence from all external
influences, the deepening Soviet involvement in the
Egyptian economy and military establishment has
tended to seriously circumscribe his freedom of action. In spite of such polemical exchanges with the
U.S.S.R. as occurred in 1959 and 1961, Nasser's willingness to return quickly to a friendly position
may well reflect the real limits of his independence.

For the U.S.S.R. has become the most important foreign source of investment for the U.A.R.'s economic
development program, the primary market for Egyptian
cotton, and the sole source of supply for the Egyptian military establishment.

The U.S.S.R., of course, has been careful to
avoid creating any serious conflict with Nasser and
apparently believes that the U.A.R.'s political and
economic policies eventually will align the U.A.R.
even more closely with the Socialist camp.   The
U.A.R.'s "positive neutralism" has suited the
U.S.S.R. because it has worked to undermine Western
interests in the Middle East and has facilitated the
introduction of a sizable Soviet presence into an
area from which it had previously been excluded.   In
no other recipient of Soviet aid has the combination
of economic and military assistance served Soviet
interests so well.   Khrushchev's visit to the U.A.R.
in 1964 and Kosygin's sojourn in 1966 highlight this
assessment.

Nasser, of course, clearly realizes that the
scope of the U.A.R.'s economic development program
also requires large-scale financial assistance from
Western sources.   The periodic moderation of U.A.R.
policies toward the West reflects the need to keep
this channel of funds open and is indicative of
Nasser's successful manipulation of regional tensions
to obtain aid from both East and West.   He undoubtedly feels that the economic interests of the U.A.R.
can be best advanced by continually stimulating such
competition and thus avoiding complete dependence
upon the U.S.S.R.

But as long as differences continue to exist
over such basic issues as Western support for Israel
and conservative Arab regimes, foreign-owned petroleum resources, and the existence of remnants of
Western colonialism in the area, no real accommoda-
tion between Nasser and the West is possible.   Nasser has not abandoned his suspicions of the West and
he believes that the West continues to oppose his
aspirations in the area.   He has not been reluctant

to risk the loss of Western aid when he feels his
major objectives being openly challenged. Without
the alternative source of military and economic aid
which the U.S.S.R. has represented, Nasser would
have been less likely to initiate actions which
might lead to a loss of Western assistance.

Notes to Chapter 5

1.   Richard Nolte, "Report on the United Arab
Republic," Middle East 1959 (Washington: Middle
East Institute, 1959), p. 26.

2.   Charles Issawi, Egypt at Mid-Century, An
Economic Survey (London: Oxford University Press,
1954), p. 102. Area under cultivation totals about
6 million acres. A large part of the area, however,
can be cultivated more than once during the year.
This fact is represented by cropped area.

3.   Royal Institute of International Affairs,
The Middle East, A Political and Economic Survey
(London: Oxford University Press, 1955), p. 216.

4.   Jean and Simonne Lacouture, Egypt in Transition, English Translation by Francis Scarfe (New
York: Criterion Books, 1958), p. 180.

5.   Quoted in The Egyptian Economic and Political Review, VII (September, 1961), 22.

6.   The New York Times, September 29, 1955, p.1.

7.   Salah El Serafy, "Economic Development by
Revolution, The Case of the UAR," The Middle East
Journal, Summer, 1963, p. 222.

8.   United Arab Republic, Statistical Pocket
Year-Book 1952-1962 (Cairo: The Administration of
Public Mobilization, 1962), p. 58.

9.   Issawi, op. cit., pp. 135-36.

10. U.N., "Government Budgets of Middle East Countries," Quarterly Bulletin of Economic Development, No. 13, April, 1958, p. 25.

11. The Egyptian Economic and Political Review (Cairo), VII (July, 1961), 5.

12. Middle East Economic Digest (London), February 5, 1960, p. 58.

13. Middle East Economist (Cairo), December, 1960, p. 12.

14. National Bank of Egypt, Economic Bulletin, No. 3 (1961), p. 279.

15. Malcolm H. Kerr, "The Emergence of a Socialist Ideology in Egypt," The Middle East Journal, XVI (Spring, 1962), 139.

16. The Egyptian Economic and Political Review VII (September, 1961), 24.

17. Economic Developments in the Middle East 1958-1959, p. 46.

18. Issawi, op. cit., p. 91.

19. U.A.R., Year Book 1959 (Cairo: Information Department, 1959), p. 87.

20. The Egyptian Gazette, May 7, 1961, p. 5.

21. Economic Developments in the Middle East 1954-1955, p. 113.

22. Economic Bulletin, No. 4 (1965), Tables 5/2-5/3.

23. Government of Egypt, Industry After the Revolution and the Five Year Plan (Cairo: Ministry of Industry, 1957), p. 97.

24. Economic Development in the Middle East 1957-1958, p. 16.

25. U.A.R., Achievements and Future Development Plans (Cairo: Information Department, 1960), p. 110.

26. Ibid., p. 169.

27. The Middle East Economist and Financial Service, IV (December, 1960), 169.

28. U.A.R., Second Five Year Plan (Cairo: Information Department, 1960), p. 159.

29. Economic Bulletin, No. 2 (1960), p. 81.

30. The Egyptian Gazette, March 7, 1960, p. 3.

31. James Davidson, "Industrialization in Egypt," The Middle East Forum, XXXVII (March, 1961), 161.

32. U.A.R., Basic Features of the Plan to Double National Income Throughout the Next Ten Years in the Southern Region of the U.A.R. (Cairo: Committee of National Planning, 1960), p. 23.

33. IBRD, The Economic Development of Egypt (Washington: 1955), p. 73.

34. U.A.R., Sadd El-Aali Project (Cairo: Information Department, 1958), pp. 15-16.

35. Government of Egypt, The Population Problem in Egypt (Cairo: The Permanent Council of Public Services, 1955), p. 22.

36. Economic Bulletin, No. 2 (1957), p. 117; No. 2 (1958), p. 98.

37. U.A.R., The Economy of the U.A.R. (Cairo: Information Department, 1960), p. 19.

38. Middle East Economist, 1-61 (January, 1961),
p. 15.

39. Basic Features of the Plan to Double National Income, p. 21.

40. The Egyptian Gazette, May 31, 1966, p. 3.

41. The Egyptian Gazette, May 2, 1966, p. 1.

42. The Egyptian Economic and Political Review, VII (January, 1961), p. XIV.

43. The Egyptian Gazette, December 25, 1960,
p. 3.

44. Charles D. Cremeans, The Arabs and the World (New York: Praeger, 1963), pp. 144-45.

45. Although the focus of this discussion is on Soviet activities, other Soviet Bloc countries are included in the aid discussion because of the important role these countries have played in Soviet policies in the U.A.R.

46. The Egyptian Economic and Political Review, IV (May, 1958), 27.

47. Davidson, op. cit., p. 159.

48. Middle East Economist and Financial Service, XIII (January, 1959), 5.

49. The Egyptian Gazette, January 6, 1960, p.3.

50. See, for example, The Egyptian Economic and Political Review, IV (May, 1958), 44-50; IV (April, 1958), 46-49; and V (February-March, 1959), 48-51 for details of the Aswan High Dam agreement and the 1958 economic aid agreement.

51. The Egyptian Gazette, December 28, 1965,
p. 3.

52.   The Egyptian Economic and Political Review,
IV (May, 1958), 45.

53.   The New York Times, February 17, 1959,
p. 4; Washington Post, June 1, 1959, p. 11;   The New
York Times, March 19, 1961, p. 56.

54.   The Middle East Observer, May 4, 1966,
p. 1.

55.   Economic Bulletin, No. 1 (1964), p. 35.

56.   The Egyptian Gazette, May 2, 1966, p. 3.

57.   The Egyptian Gazette, May 15, 1966, p. 3.

58.   The Middle East Observer, May 19, 1965,
p. 1.

6

Economic assistance has become an important weapon in the foreign policy arsenals of both the U.S. and the U.S.S.R. Because economic aid has become an integral component of American and Soviet foreign policy, it is likely to be maintained at a high level for some time to come. And while some favorable returns from these programs have accrued to both countries, the foundations for achieving their long-run objectives are far from being established. In most less developed countries, prospects for achieving self-sustaining growth--the primary objective of the U.S. aid program--still do not appear favorable. For the U.S.S.R., the goal of escorting its aid recipients along the "noncapitalist path to socialism" has begun to encounter many rocky obstacles which have necessitated periodic ideological manipulations to justify the continuation of economic aid to "bourgeois-nationalist" regimes.

CONTRIBUTION TO ECONOMIC DEVELOPMENT

Although the pattern of foreign economic assistance to Turkey, India, and the U.A.R. has differed, such aid has contributed to their economic growth and has assisted in expanding output in those sectors into which it has been channeled. During the past fifteen years, official donations have made sizable contributions to capital formation in these countries. U.S. aid expenditures during the respective development plans have comprised 17 per cent of total investment in Turkey, 16 per cent in India, and about 25 per cent of total investment in the U.A.R. Soviet outlays during a nine-year period accounted for less than 5 per cent of total investment

166

in India's industrial sector, or less than 2 per
cent of total investment. Soviet bloc outlays for
the U.A.R.'s five-year plan represented about 13 per
cent of total investment. Aid expenditures by the
U.S. added between one-fifth and one-seventh to the
level of gross savings in the three countries.
Soviet bloc outlays in the U.A.R. probably increased
domestic savings about 15 per cent.

In the absence of economic assistance, particularly U.S. aid, it is unlikely that any of the three
countries would have experienced any significant increase in national income. The few years of most
rapid economic growth in Turkey and India occurred
with relatively little economic aid. Large-scale
aid began to flow into these countries after their
development programs appeared to be stagnating.
Without such aid, the tempo of development would have
declined drastically.

Turkey experienced a short period of real and
substantial growth between 1950 and 1954. For India
this situation prevailed during the first plan. In
both countries, fortuitous circumstances contributed
substantially to their achievements and foreign economic assistance was relatively unimportant. After
1953, the rate of Turkish economic growth declined;
real per capita income rose about one per cent annually through 1959. This stagnation prevailed despite
the increasing magnitude of U.S. economic assistance.
The size of U.S. aid approximated nearly three-
fourths of the real increase in Turkey's GNP during
the 1950's. If U.S. economic aid had not been available, investment would have declined by at least the
amount of aid and per capita income would have
dropped sharply.

The increase in national income of 18.4 per
cent during India's first plan was accomplished with
a relatively small amount of foreign economic assistance. The real increase in national income of 25
per cent during the second plan required a rise of
135 per cent in total domestic expenditures. Foreign
economic assistance experienced a sixfold increase,
rising from about $395 million to $2.3 billion. By

the end of the fourth year of the third plan, an
additional $5.2 billion had been used. During the
first plan, 43 per cent of the foreign aid used (ex-
cluding agricultural commodities) was expended for
agricultural development and 5 per cent for industrial development. The shares spent in these sectors during the second plan were sharply reversed--
9 per cent in agriculture and 35 per cent in industry.

The amount of U.S. aid used for the first plan
(about $350 million) consisted mainly of agricultural
commodities and goods and technical services provided
under various technical assistance programs. During
the second plan, $3.4 billion was spent from avail-
able U.S. aid commitments. The bulk of these funds
was used for general commodity imports and technical
assistance.

This growing dependence on foreign assistance
on the part of many developing countries is rather
disconcerting because a sizable (and, perhaps, growing) share of new aid commitments have been channeled into nonproject assistance necessary to keep
these economies operating at a relatively high level.
Consequently, an increasing share of the external
debt burden of these countries represents repayment
for aid not used to expand productive facilities and
will create future serious balance-of-payments difficulties. While the U.S.S.R. has not provided such
assistance (except to other Communist countries), it
may be compelled to do so to protect large aid investments, particularly in the U.A.R.

SECTORAL DISTRIBUTION OF AID

In general, Western economic theory has held
that in the early stages of economic development,
emphasis should be placed on agricultural and infrastructural development. But while the U.S. has encouraged such emphasis and has channeled large
amounts of capital into the development of transportation, communication, and electric power facilities,
aid for agriculture has been insufficient. Nearly
60 per cent of U.S. aid outlays in Turkey, for

example, were expended for industrial, mining, and related electric power facilities. The agricultural sector received only 6 per cent of total U.S. aid expenditures. Despite U.S. aid outlays totaling TL 7 billion, accounting for 31 per cent of gross investment, the industrial sector accounted for only 10 per cent of the increase in national income. Moreover, its annual contribution to total national income has remained relatively constant.

The Soviet bloc has been providing economic assistance for the U.A.R.'s economic development since 1957, but the bulk of this aid has been consciously directed toward the industrial sector. Except for about $400 million in Communist aid commitments, all allocations have been for the expansion of industrial facilities. Soviet aid to India has been almost completely for industrial development.

The pattern of Soviet aid to India and the U.A.R., however, tends to bias the sectoral distribution of aid to all Soviet aid recipients. About two-thirds of Soviet commitments for the construction of industrial facilities have been undertaken in these two countries, as well as the overwhelming share of heavy industrial undertakings. In other Soviet aid recipients, the projects undertaken generally are conditioned by the resources available in these countries. In Afghanistan, for example, about half of Soviet aid has been allocated for the construction of transportation facilities. Substantial sums have been obligated for the development of mineral resources and the construction of multipurpose projects. Manufacturing units being constructed with Soviet aid are small and require simple skills for their operation. It is incorrect to suggest, as one author has, that, based on selected examples:

> There is an incipient pattern of international specialization. . . . When a country wants assistance for its small industries, it is more likely to turn to Japan, the Scandinavian countries and the United States rather than the Soviet Union. . . . Similarly, when

it comes to improving peasant agriculture, the Soviet Union would be an unlikely assistant. But if aid for resource exploration or large industry in
the government sector is desired, American disinterest (or dislike) and Russian
sympathy is apt to attract Soviet assistance.[1]

AID TO THE PUBLIC SECTOR

One of the primary objectives the U.S.S.R. seeks
to achieve with its aid program is the expansion of
the public sector in recipient countries. Furthermore, such aid frequently has been made available
for investment in undertakings in which the private
sector had the dominant role. A sizable part of
Soviet aid to India has been allocated for such traditional preserves of private interests as petroleum
and pharmaceuticals. Soviet aid to the U.A.R. not
only has become the major foreign source of assistance for the latter's development program but has
supported the U.A.R.'s nationalization measures.

One of the important stated objectives of the
U.S. aid program has been the development of political and economic frameworks in recipient countries
conducive to the rapid growth of their private sectors. But the bulk of U.S. economic assistance has
been channeled into the public sector. Probably not
more than 15 per cent of U.S. aid to Turkey and 10
per cent of U.S. assistance to India was directly
allocated to the private sector. Practically all of
the assistance provided to the U.A.R. has been for
use by the public sector.

While much has been made of the relatively
small sums of U.S. aid flowing into the private sector, it is not meant to imply that U.S. aid is assisting the U.S.S.R. to achieve its objective of dis-
placing the private sector. What this analysis has
sought to point out is that the volume of aid to private interests is not in accordance with our stated
objectives. It often is unfortunate that, in the

need to justify the aid program, U.S. officials
often must highlight objectives which are not likely to be achieved to the extent or in the time ref-
erence indicated. Although the larger share of U.S.
aid flows toward the public sector, much of this aid
is being used for the development of infrastructure,
e.g., transportation and electric power, facilities
which help to create conditions conducive to private
investment. Moreover, in all developing countries
the state usually is the only one capable of undertaking such development.

On the other hand, the economic assistance provided by the U.S.S.R. to most developing countries
also goes into infrastructural development and also
assists in the creation of conditions favorable for
new private investment, as well as strengthening the
ability of recipients to pursue non-Communist paths
to development. In as remote a place as Yemen, the
construction of a port at Hodeidah greatly stimulated
business in that city. Moreover, the need to deal
with local private subcontractors on Soviet projects
also provides a stimulant for private business.

Most developing countries are nationalistic and
socialistic in outlook. The leaders of these countries believe that the government must play the key
role in a more equitable distribution of the domestic product. Some governments are politically committed to socialistic solutions for their basic economic problems. To a large extent the deep involvement of the government in economic activities results from the lack of natural and human resources,
the absence of an entrepreneurial class, and the vul-
nerability to external political and economic pressures. Their unwillingness to permit a larger role
for foreign private investment frequently stems from
an association of all private investment with exploi-
tation.

Under these conditions, an economic system in
which private enterprise determines the course of development cannot be expected to evolve in the near
future. The factors which contributed to Western
economic development find few parallels in the

developing countries. The system of free and private enterprise which has prevailed in the West has found it difficult to take root in the institutions of these countries. Moreover, their prevailing environmental framework has spawned the predilection for strong central governments, the "strong man," and centralized direction of economic activities. The practical policy which can be pursued under such conditions is to work within the framework of the recipient country's political and economic institutions. The techniques and methods the other country employs often may not coincide with the forms we think best. But the choice for many countries is not between a free enterprise or socialist system but one which will enable them to solve their economic problems within a non-Communist framework.

It is probable that foreign private investment will again be welcome in those countries in which the public sector has become dominant. The form of this investment, however, often is not likely to be the traditional form.   It may have to join in ventures with capital provided by the host government and/or private interests in the recipient country. Such arrangements already exist in many developing countries. Also, credits for the sale of capital goods and for construction of projects can be provided under credit guarantee programs. West Germany, Japan, and Italy are engaged in a variety of activities under such programs. To encourage U.S. investment in this direction, AID has vigorously pressed its investment guaranty program. By the end of 1964, such agreements had been concluded with sixty-three countries covering $1.8 billion in U.S. investments.[2]

TERMS OF REPAYMENT

An important consideration for a developing country seeking capital for economic development is the terms of repayment for borrowed capital. For an extended period of time, the capital requirements of the developing countries will exceed their ability to repay such capital. The actual amount of

debt that can be serviced will depend largely on the
terms of debt repayment. The future burden of current obligations can affect the future rate of economic development if these obligations impose a
heavy drain on a country's financial resources.

For many developing countries whose creditworthiness is limited, prospects are dim for sizable
imports of capital goods on regular commercial terms.
Some countries, e.g., Turkey, borrowed heavily in
the early years of their development programs. The
obligations that accumulated are of such magnitude
that additional large-scale borrowings on convention-
al terms are precluded. If assistance from foreign
official sources was not available as an alternative,
or additional, source of funds, the prospects for
meaningful economic development in many countries
would not be bright. The threat to external liquid-
ity could be critical at a time when many developing
countries are struggling for political survival.

An important difference between the aid programs
of the U.S. and the U.S.S.R. is the terms under which
such aid is provided. Almost all Soviet assistance
is extended in the form of credits repayable in
twelve years beginning one year after delivery of
all machinery and equipment. Interest on Soviet
credits usually is 2.5 per cent. Rarely is Soviet
aid provided as a grant. Payment of principal and
interest generally is in the form of commodities
usually exported by the recipient countries.

The bulk of U.S. aid has been provided as grants
or as loans repayable in local currency. As such,
they impose no long-term repayment burden on recipient countries. Terms on U.S. loans vary with the
lending organization. MSP and DLF loan repayment
periods range from 3-40 years with grace periods of
1-7 years. Export-Import Bank loans call for repayment periods averaging 7 years. Interest charges on
all loans have ranged between 0.75-6 per cent.

Despite the lower interest charges on Soviet
credits, the longer repayment periods of AID loans
impose less of a burden on the economies of countries

receiving such aid. This is particularly true of
loans repayable in local currencies. Furthermore,
the U.S. has been willing to revise initial repayment terms when the aid recipient is in financial
difficulties. Both India and Turkey have been
beneficiaries of postponed payments. There is no
evidence that the U.S.S.R. has been as magnanimous
with repayment of its economic aid.

THE P.L. 480 PROGRAM

The dispensation of agricultural commodities
under the P.L. 480 program has become a mainstay of
the U.S. aid program. For countries with large-
scale development programs and rapidly increasing
population, aid in the form of food helps to ease
the drain on foreign-exchange reserves, lessens inflationary pressures, and often increases the general level of food consumption. In most countries
receiving economic aid, food supplies are inadequate.
The initiation of development activities increases
incomes, a large part of which are spent on food.
Owing to the difficulties of raising the level of
agricultural production rapidly, these countries are
compelled to spend part of their foreign-exchange
earnings on the import of food. The local currencies
which accumulate from the sale of these agricultural
commodities are then loaned or granted to the recipient country and serve as a noninflationary form of
finance. New money is not created but money previously withdrawn from circulation reenters the economy.
In effect, the commodities which generated the deposits become grants. These currencies, however, do
not represent an addition to the country's real resources as the deposits still represent claims on
the country's domestic resources.

An important consideration concerning the P.L.
480 program is that by making agricultural commodities more plentiful, the recipient country may de-
vote less resources to agricultural development and
more to other sectors. The sectoral pattern of investment in India and Turkey may reflect just such a
situation since both countries continue to place

greater emphasis on industrial development. The
availability of large sums of local currencies also
may have an effect on the fiscal policies of the recipient country. Most developing countries are reluctant to devise more equitable tax structures
which would tax the politically powerful agricultural
and commercial interests. This has been the case in
Turkey. One prerequisite initially imposed on Turkey
before a consortium would agree to support that country's current development program was the institution of a more effective tax structure.

A problem of growing concern, however, is that
the demand for U.S. surpluses is growing and projected requirements during the next decade may well
exceed the ability of the U.S. to meet the demand.
Countries receiving such assistance must be convinced
of the wisdom of investing larger sums to expand agricultural output even if it results in a reduction of
the rate of industrial investment. It is for this
reason that early in 1966, President Johnson called
for a five-year, $3.5 billion program to help expand
agricultural production in developing countries.[3]
To encourage others to seriously concern themselves
with agricultural investment and to reduce the enor-
mous sums of local currencies accumulated, most of
future P.L. 480 assistance may require dollar payments.[4]

POLITICAL CONSIDERATIONS

The U.S. objective of employing economic aid to
help generate self-sustaining economic growth under
democratic and politically stable governments seems
as far from attainment as it was in 1950. In spite
of the large sum of U.S. economic assistance provided
to the developing countries, none of the recipients
has achieved a position enabling it to dispense with
economic aid. Furthermore, political instability
continues to be a prevailing characteristic in almost all developing countries receiving economic
aid. But while the lack of visible achievement is
frustrating, we are, after all, concerned with a
process that cannot be accomplished in a few decades.

It took the Western world centuries to achieve the
stage of economic growth it currently enjoys. Our
aid still has enabled many developing countries to
continue to grapple with their economic problems
while avoiding the political turmoil favorable for
direct Communist involvement.

The short-run objectives of the Soviet aid program have been easier to achieve and, consequently,
the U.S.S.R. has been more successful in employing
economic assistance for policy objectives. Starting
from a position of little influence, the immediate
objective was to achieve recognition as a major
power. The willingness of many developing countries
to accept Soviet political, economic, and military
support enabled the Soviet Union to interject itself
into areas in which it had little influence prior to
1955. As a result of its aid program, the U.S.S.R.
has been able to establish a strong presence across
the belt of developing countries ranging from Cuba
to Indonesia, changing the previously prevailing
Soviet image from a menacing scowl to an almost be-
nevolent smile. The Soviet aid program also has
broadened what used to be an exceedingly narrow base
of communications between the U.S.S.R. and the developing countries, whose emergence is now regarded
by the Soviet Union as being of decisive importance
to the future course of world history. Soviet support for the nationalist movements in many of these
countries has been an important factor in weakening,
or eliminating, Western influence in such diverse
areas as Indonesia, the Middle East, and Cuba.

It is part of the U.S.S.R.'s long-run objectives
to convince the non-Western world that Communism
offers the only means for rapid economic growth.
Soviet technical assistance programs seek to instill
a preference for Soviet-type institutions. In spite
of the larger number of students from developing
countries studying in the West, the new élite in
many countries is increasingly becoming Soviet
trained. Moreover, students trained in the West and
influenced by Western political and economic doctrines are not likely to be placed in positions of
authority in governmental organizations which operate contrary to those doctrines.

The latter point is particularly significant where the military is concerned, for many countries are controlled by military hierarchies. Military training for their personnel in the U.S.S.R. generally cannot be balanced by similar training in the West. In the Middle East, the military groups historically have been a major source of authority. The earliest indication of Western influence was evident in the organization of the military. The effect of present Soviet training on future military leaders may be expected to influence to some degree the political and economic orientation of these trainees.

Although much of the difficulties encountered in generating the required growth forces is a result of economic, social, and political institutions which are slow to change, some of the fault lies with U.S. aid policies. This was true, for example, during the period when security was the primary determinant of aid recipients. Under such circumstances, economic development became a secondary consideration and the effectiveness of aid expenditures tended to be dissipated. In a country such as Turkey, defense support and military aid outlays contributed to inflationary pressures during the mid-1950's and permitted much wasteful use of aid funds. Of course, in situations where open Communist aggression is involved, as in Viet Nam, there is no choice but to relegate development to a secondary position.

Economic aid as a weapon in the Cold War previously had done much to distort the aid programs. Within this framework, it is inevitable that the selection of aid institutions, aid recipients, aid criteria, and types of aid will be influenced more by political than by economic considerations. In many instances, economic assistance has been provided to countries other than those that could utilize such aid most efficiently and for purposes not likely to maximize economic growth.

The possibility that any developing country, given the proper political and economic conditions, might accept economic aid from any source projected

all developing countries into the forefront of the
Cold War. Some leaders used the conflict to pursue
regional objectives, penalize former colonial powers,
or strengthen their position within their countries.
In other countries, e.g., the U.A.R., Ghana, and
Guinea, Soviet economic assistance has been used, in
part, to initiate rapid and widespread economic and
social changes.

There are, in general, certain obligations which
recipient countries are expected to fulfill. Economic
development and economic aid programs must be accompanied by sound fiscal and monetary policies within
the framework of comprehensive economic programs.
Moreover, it is expected that recipients will institute and implement vigorously social and economic
reforms. The U.S. cannot, of course, demand that a
country's development program and economic institutions follow a particular pattern. Nationalization
of privately owned assets and initiation of policies
designed to expand the public sector are likely to
occur in a number of countries. But these developments alone should not determine subsequent U.S.
economic aid policy. The key factor should be a
country's political orientation.

One problem prevailing in almost all developing
countries which must be alleviated is the rapid increase in population. The rate of population growth
in many of these countries approaches or exceeds 2.5
per cent a year, and in some it is over 3 per cent.
In the Western world, population growth followed or
accompanied economic development. In the developing
countries today, rapid population growth is preceding economic development. Consequently, capital and
current output, which could otherwise be employed to
raise standards of living, has to be used instead
for meeting the economic and social needs of this increase in population.

PROSPECTS FOR THE AID PROGRAMS

The future of the U.S. program is clouded by
domestic and international political factors. Domestically, there is a growing impatience with the lack
of any visible achievements in the developing countries. Such impatience is intensified by the unwillingness of many recipient countries to undertake the
necessary economic, social, and fiscal reforms and
by the occasional "go to hell with your aid." U.S.
balance-of-payments problems and the reluctance of
the European countries to expand significantly their
aid programs add further to the domestic criticism
of the aid program. At a time when many developing
countries require larger amounts of aid to maintain
the momentum of their aid programs, the size of U.S.
aid appropriations has tended to decline. India's
fourth plan, for example, calls for total outlays of
$47.5 billion, double those of the third plan and
three times as large as the second plan. But in
spite of the annual hurdles that the aid program
must overcome, it is likely to continue at a relatively high level because it remains a useful and
necessary component of U.S. foreign policy.

The U.S.S.R. also faces problems not unlike
those of the U.S. The Sino-Soviet conflict has
exacerbated the ideological dilemma of aiding
"national bourgeois" governments, particularly at
the expense of Communist groups in these countries.
The Soviet Union also has had to exercise restraint
over the treatment of Communists in the Middle East
and the periodic anti-Soviet outbursts of Nasser.
In spite of the large amounts of military and economic aid extended to Indonesia, the Sukarno regime
preferred to pursue pro-Chinese policies. At times
like these, or during periods of economic difficulties in the U.S.S.R., the Stalinist elements tend to
become more vocal and point to the lack of political
returns from their aid program.

OUTLOOK FOR THE SOVIET AID PROGRAM

The U.S.S.R. also has had to assess the returns of its aid program. Although the short-run objectives were largely achieved, the road along which the Soviet Union believes it must travel to attain its long-run goals has become tortuous. The decline in Western influence in many areas has not necessarily led to a corresponding rise in Soviet influence. The new governments generally have converted their anticolonialist energies into strongly assertive nationalist policies directed toward their own objectives. The surge of nationalism has also led to various regional movements, such as pan-Arabism and pan-Africanism, which the U.S.S.R. has viewed as incompatible with its long-range interests in these areas.

The U.S.S.R. also has had to accept the fall of such pro-Soviet leaders as Ben Bella, Kassem, and Nkrumah. Not only has the U.S.S.R. had to accept the loss of the political and economic investment in those countries, but it also has had to bear the onus of its close association with the deposed regimes. Nevertheless, economic aid also has become too much a part of Soviet foreign policy and it will continue to follow its present pattern for some time to come. The Soviet Union must preserve the political advantages already won and is unlikely to curtail significantly a program which has proven to be one of Moscow's most effective weapons in its struggle for influence in Asia and Africa, both in competition with the West and with Communist China.

But, just as with the U.S., the U.S.S.R. is bound to discover that past large-scale investments require even larger sums to maintain positions already gained. The greatest return for the Soviet Union has come from such countries as the U.A.R., with its radical anti-Western policies and unyielding socialism. In such cases, however, Soviet economic and military aid has encouraged overspending on the part of the recipient. Yet the U.S.S.R. has not been willing to provide the assistance required

to ease the subsequent balance-of-payments difficulties or to provide the local-cost financing to prevent domestic inflationary financing. In a country
like the U.A.R., it seems quite probable that the
U.S.S.R. will have to come forth with the type of
nonproject aid the U.S. has had to provide to keep
such economies operating at a relatively high level.

Notes to Chapter 6

1. Comparisons of the United States and Soviet
Economies, p. 170.

2. U.S. Department of State and Department of
Defense, Proposed Mutual Defense and Development Programs FY 1966 (Washington: 1965), p. 9.

3. The New York Times, February 9, 1966, p. 1.

4. It was estimated that by the end of 1966,
the U.S. would have accumulated some $12 billion in
the local currency for its own use. See U.S. Department of State, The Problem of Excess Accumulation of
U.S.-Owned Local Currencies, Report of the Consultants
on International Finance and Economic Problems, April
4, 1960, App. I, p. 1.

SELECTED BIBLIOGRAPHY

SELECTED BIBLIOGRAPHY

Official Publications

India

Ministry of Finance. Economic Survey, Annual issues.
     Delhi, 1961-66.

Ministry of Information and Broadcasting. India
     1965. Delhi, 1965.

Planning Commission. First Five Year Plan. Delhi,
     1953.

_____. Review of the First Five Year Plan. New
     Delhi, 1957.

_____. Second Five Year Plan. New Delhi, 1956.

_____. Third Five Year Plan. New Delhi, 1961.

_____. Third Five Year Plan, A Draft Outline.
     New Delhi, 1960.

Turkey

Central Statistical Office. National Income of
     Turkey. Ankara, 1960-62.

Industrial Development Bank of Turkey. Annual
     Statement. Ankara, 1956-64.

Organization for International Cooperation. Quar-
     terly Report on the Marshall Plan in Turkey.
     Ankara, 1950-57.

State Planning Organization. First Five-Year Devel-
     opment Plan of Turkey 1963-1967. Ankara, 1963.

United Arab Republic

Information Department. Achievements and Future De-
    velopment Plans. Cairo, 1960.

Ministry of Industry. Industry After the Revolution
    and the Five Year Plan. Cairo, 1957.

United States

Commission on Foreign Economic Policy. Report to
    the President and the Congress. Washington,
    1954.

Composite Report of the President's Committee to
    Study the United States Military Assistance
    Program. Washington, 1957.

Congress, Joint Economic Committee. Comparisons of
    the United States and Soviet Economies. Papers
    Submitted to Subcommittee on Economic Statis-
    tics, 86th Cong., 1st Sess. Washington, 1959.

_____, Senate Committee on Foreign Relations.
    Foreign Aid. Report of Special Subcommittee,
    85th Cong., 1st Sess. Washington, 1957.

_____. The Objectives of United States Economic
    Assistance Programs. Study Prepared by Massa-
    chusetts Institute of Technology for the Spe-
    cial Subcommittee to Study the Foreign Aid
    Program, 85th Cong., 1st Sess. Washington,
    1957.

_____. Technical Assistance. Report of Commit-
    tee, 85th Cong., 1st Sess. Washington, 1957.

Department of Agriculture, Foreign Agricultural Ser-
    vice. Agricultural Development in Turkey. Re-
    port No. 106. Washington, 1958.

Department of State. Communist Economic Policy in
    the Less Developed Areas. Publication No. 7020.
    Washington, 1960.

_____. The Communist Economic Threat. Publica-
tion No. 6777. Washington, 1959.

_____. The Problem of Excess Accumulation of
U.S.-Owned Local Currencies. Reports of the
Consultants on International Finance and Prob-
lems. April 4, 1960.

_____. The Sino-Soviet Bloc Economic Offensive
Through 1964. Research Memorandum. August 4,
1965.
        .

_____. The Sino-Soviet Economic Offensive in the
Less Developed Countries. Publication No. 6632.
Washington, 1958.

_____. The Threat of Soviet Economic Policy.
Publication No. 7234. Washington, 1961.

International Organizations

Food and Agriculture Organization. FAO Mediterranean Development Project. Rome, 1959.

International Bank for Reconstruction and Development. The Economic Development of Egypt.
Washington, 1955.

_____. The Economy of Turkey. Baltimore: Johns
Hopkins University Press, 1951.

United Nations, Department of Economic and Social
Affairs. Economic Developments in the Middle
East. New York, 1955-64.

Books

Asher, Robert E. Grants, Loans, and Local Currencies, Their Role in Foreign Aid. Washington:
The Brookings Institution, 1961.

Aubrey, Henry G. Coexistence: Economic Challenge
    and Response. Washington: National Planning
    Association, 1961.

Bauer, P. T. United States Aid and Indian Economic
    Development. Washington: American Enterprise
    Association, 1959.

Berliner, Joseph S. Soviet Economic Aid. New York:
    Frederick A. Praeger, Inc., 1958.

Bhattacharyya, Dhiresh. India's Five Year Plan.
    Calcutta: Mdayan Granthagar, 1962.

Billerbeck, Klaus. Soviet Bloc Foreign Aid to the
    Underdeveloped Countries. Hamburg: Hamburg
    Archives of World Economy, 1960.

Choudhury, Radharani. The Plans for Economic Devel-
    opment in India. Calcutta: Bookland Private
    Ltd., 1959.

Cremeans, Charles D. The Arabs and the World. New
    York: Frederick A. Praeger, 1963.

Frank, Peter G. Afghanistan Between East and West.
    Washington: National Planning Association,
    1960.

Gadgil, D. R. Planning and Economic Policy in India.
    Poona, India: Gokale Institute of Politics and
    Economics, 1961.

Grunwald, Kurt, and Ronall, Joachim O. Industrial-
    ization in the Middle East. New York: Council
    for Middle Eastern Affairs Press, 1960.

Gulati, I. S. Resource Prospects of the Third Five
    Year Plan. Bombay: Orient Longmans Private,
    Ltd., 1960.

Hald, Marjorie W. The Export-Import Bank and Devel-
    opment Lending. Santa Monica: The Rand Corpo-
    ration, 1959.

Hershlag, Z. Y. Turkey: An Economy in Transition.
    The Hague: Van Keulen, 1958.

Higgins, Benjamin. Economic Development. New York:
    W. W. Norton & Company, 1959.

Indian Merchants' Chamber. National Income of India.
    Bombay: Economic Research and Training Founda-
    tion, 1963.

Issawi, Charles. Egypt at Mid-Century, An Economic
    Survey. London: Oxford University Press, 1959.

_____. Egypt in Revolution; An Economic Analysis.
    London: Oxford University Press, 1963.

Kovner, Milton. The Challenge of Coexistence. Wash-
    ington: Public Affairs Press, 1961.

Lacouture, Jean and Simonne. Egypt Transition.
    Translated by Francis Scarfe. New York: Cri-
    terion Books, 1958.

Lewis, John P. Quiet Crisis in India, Economic De-
    velopment and American Policy. Washington:
    The Brookings Institution, 1962.

Little, Tom. High Dam at Aswan. New York: The
    John Day Company, 1965.

Malenbaum, Wilfred. East and West in India's Devel-
    opment. Washington: National Planning Associ-
    ation, 1959.

Price, Harry Bayard. The Marshall Plan and Its
    Meaning. Ithaca: Cornell University Press,
    1955.

Rao, V.K.R.V., and Narain, Dharm. Foreign Aid and
    India's Economic Development. Bombay: Insti-
    tute of Economic Growth, 1963.

Royal Institute of International Affairs. The Middle
    East, A Political and Economic Survey. London:
    Oxford University Press, 1955.

Sapir, Michael. The New Role of the Soviets in the
     World Economy. New York: Committee for Eco-
     nomic Development, April, 1958.

Upadhyaya, Deendayal. The Two Plans: Promises, Per-
     formance, Prospects. Lucknow: Rashtradberma
     Prakachan Ltd., 1958.

                    Periodicals

"Communist Traders Look Ahead," East Europe, XII
     (December, 1959), 19-27.

Dajani, Burhan. "American and Soviet Aid, A Com-
     parison," Middle East Forum, XXXVI (June,
     1960), 15-17.

Davidson, James. "Industrialization in Egypt,"
     Middle East Forum, XXXVII (March, 1961),
     161-62.

"The Democratic Party Election Manifesto," Middle
     Eastern Affairs, I (May, 1950), 149-50.

Diab, Muhammad. "The Economic System of the U.A.R.
     Where Is It Going?" Middle East Forum, XXXVII
     (June, 1961), 14-20.

"India 1960, A Survey of Economic Progress Since
     1947," Far Eastern Economic Review, February 4,
     1960, pp. 153-64.

Iren, Cihat. "Foreign Capital Investment in Turkey,"
     Turkish Economic Review, I (February, 1960),
     3-7.

Kerr, Malcolm H. "The Emergence of a Socialist
     Ideology in Egypt," Middle East Journal, XVI
     (Spring, 1962).

Mannin, Ethel. "Nasser and His Socialism," Middle
     East Forum, XL (February–March, 1964), 17-21.

Master, M. A.   "External Assistance for Five Year
    Plans," The Asian Economic Review, III (May,
    1961), 219-32.

Nicholls, W. H. "Investment in Agriculture in Under-
    developed Countries," American Economic Review,
    XLV (May, 1955), 58-72.

Nielsen, Waldemar A., and Hodjera, Zoran S.   "Sino-
    Soviet Bloc Technical Assistance--Another Bi-
    lateral Approach," The Annals, CCCXXIII (May,
    1959), 40-49.

Nove, A.   "The Soviet Model and Underdeveloped Coun-
    tries," International Affairs (London), XXXVII
    (January, 1961), 29-38.

Ohly, John H.   "Competitive Aspects of Foreign Aid,"
    SRI Journal, III (Fourth Quarter, 1959), 173-78.

Okyar, Osman.   "Economic Framework for Industrializa-
    tion, Turkish Experiences in Retrospect," Middle
    Eastern Affairs, IX (August-September, 1958),
    261-67.

_____.   "The Turkish Stabilization Experiment--
    Before and After," Middle Eastern Affairs, XI
    (August-September, 1960), 238-46.

Pettengill, Robert.   "Economic System of the U.A.R.
    How Is It Going?" Middle East Forum, XXXVII
    (September, 1961), 39-42.

Rosenstein-Rodan, P. N.   "International Aid for
    Underdeveloped Countries," The Review of Eco-
    nomics and Statistics, XLIII (May, 1961),
    107-38.

Rymalov, V.   "Economic Competition of the Two Sys-
    tems and the Problem of Aid to Underdeveloped
    Countries," Problems of Economics, III (Decem-
    ber, 1960), 43-52.

Sarma, N. A. "Economic Development in India: The
    First and Second Five Year Plans," <u>International
    Monetary Fund Staff Papers</u>, VI (April, 1958),
    180-238.

Scott, N. B. "Soviet Economic Relations with the
    Under-Developed Countries," <u>Soviet Studies</u>,
    X (July, 1958), 36-53.

ABOUT THE AUTHOR

Leo Tansky has been a U.S. government economist since 1952. During 1953-55, he served as a specialist on the international economic relations of Communist countries. Since 1955, he has devoted his attention to the problems of economic development of the less-developed countries, with particular emphasis on their relations with the Communist world.

Dr. Tansky has traveled and studied in the Middle East. He holds a B.S. degree from Syracuse University, an M.S. from Columbia University, and a Ph.D. degree from American University.